Praise for *Death and its Terrible, Horrible,*
No Good, Very Beautiful Lessons

"Having lost my father when I was eight years old and then never dealing with that grief, Becky's book feels like the book I wish I'd had as a child. I can't go back in time so I'll read it again and again and give it to anyone I know who may need it. Which is to say: all humans."

—Jennifer Pastiloff, bestselling author of *On Being Human*

"In her transformative book *Death and its Terrible, Horrible, No Good, Very Beautiful Lessons*, Becky Aud-Jennison takes our hand and walks us into the beautiful, horrible realm of dying and grief. Through the wisdom she has garnered from her own losses and from the stories of *The Death Dialogues Project*, Becky shows us that the awe-full journey of grief is unique to each person but is ultimately traveled by everyone. Read this marvelous book to discover that Death is the ultimate maker of change and meaning in life and to embrace both the beauty and the pain of this human existence."

—Karen Wyatt MD, author of *7 Lessons for Living from the Dying*; host of End-of-Life University Podcast

"From the very first sentence of this luminous book, filled with hard and tender truths, Becky Aud-Jennison takes the reader by the hand: 'See, death isn't so awful. You don't have to be afraid. Let's explore its hills and valleys together.' This book of 'conversations you might not find elsewhere' is a precious gem. Thank you, Becky Aud-Jennison for generously sharing the work of your heart and soul. I now have the perfect gift to give anyone who is grieving, facing death, or walking the razor's edge between this world and the next. This compassion-filled book is a gift and a treasure."

—Laura Davis, author of *The Burning Light of Two Stars* and *The Courage to Heal*

"*Death and Its Terrible, Horrible, No Good, Beautiful Lessons* is a heart touching, mind opening book of stories, ideas, and food for thought about a subject most people run away from. Don't run from this one, you'll miss a lighted path of a feared, not talked about topic. A tender read!"

—Barbara Karnes, RN, Award winning End of Life Educator

"This book is thoughtful, well put together, and beautifully written. I think it will bring comfort to many and be thought-provoking for others. I've been in this somewhat altered universe since 2011, lost five family members in six years, been as I put it 'decimated' or 'taken down to the studs' and still I learned some new things from your book that furthered my own personal healing. The power of dialogue and the power of the written word. Wow! You have done a wonderful thing with this project."

—Heike Mertins, author of *Grief Is…Thoughts on Loss, Struggle, and New Beginnings*

Death and its Terrible, Horrible,

No Good, Very Beautiful Lessons

Field Notes from
The Death Dialogues Project

Becky Aud-Jennison

Published by Motina Books, LLC, Van Alstyne, Texas
www.MotinaBooks.com

Library of Congress Cataloguing-in-Publication Data:
Names: Aud-Jennison, Becky
Title: Death and Its Terrible, Horrible, No Good, Very Beautiful Lessons
Description: First Edition. | Van Alstyne: Motina Books, 2022

Identifiers:
LCCN: 2021949470

ISBN-13: 978-1-945060-35-9 (paperback)
ISBN-13: 978-1-945060-34-2 (e-book)
ISBN-13: 978-1-945060-36-6 (hardcover)

Subjects: BISAC:
Nonfiction>Self-Help>Death, Grief, Bereavement
Nonfiction>Social Science Death & Dying

Cover Design and Images – Felicia Olin
Interior Design – Diane Windsor

this book is dedicated
to the dead whose names were never again spoken
and
to the storytellers of this project who refuse to be silent

let us begin

tell me your story

and I'll tell you mine

we will meet in the field

where love lives

as if we were yet to know loss

and dream together of how

we are to live without them

Welcome.

I'm so pleased you have found this place, where we speak of death openly, and I'm gutted for you if overwhelming heartbreak sent you looking. My wish is that your relationship with death becomes a kinder, gentler experience for coming here.

Maybe you are on the heels of great, traumatic loss.

Maybe someone in your life is experiencing deep grief and you are looking for ways to be a better human for them.

Maybe death, itself, keeps you up at night; worrying about its eventual knock on your door.

And quite possibly, you are intrigued with the stage of life we call death and dying, and opening these pages falls within the many ways you wish to expand your understanding of death and begin to walk hand in hand with it.

For whatever reason you are here: Welcome.

You belong here.

Welcome to this garden of messy, overgrown, yet frequently beautiful weeds.

There are books on death, dying, and grief aplenty—*so why read this one?*

Soon after experiencing the unimaginable, people repeatedly say they go searching, wanting to hear from the people who have been there. Many survivors say they want to witness that someone could actually live through this heart-wrenching pain they are experiencing. And just maybe, along the way as they explore others' stories, they will be given hope for moving forward.

Within *The Death Dialogues Project*, we have had countless conversations surrounding death. Not all of *the real* gets published or brought into the light in mainstream publications.

What you'll find here is the steam escaping from a pot full of conversations, sometimes boiling and sometimes simmering slowly, a stew of experiences, concerns and questions from people looking over death's abyss.

Maybe you can envision the typical book on the topic of death as neatly poured pavement, and this offering as the weeds that grow up through the cracks—straggly, thorny, sometimes blossoming, difficult to yank out and ever-returning.

This book holds conversations that you may not find elsewhere. Jagged edges, unanswered questions, and cloistered observations.

This book was created to hold you.

the death dialogues project's "why"

Why, oh why, have humans run from death to the point that we have rendered ourselves mute in its presence?

The answers are many and vast and frequently remain deeply buried.

Fear.

Escape.

Superstition.

Denial.

Discomfort.

Illiteracy surrounding the end of life and death.

Viewing death as failure.

Fear, however, seems to be the common thread woven through all of these reasons. Fear often leads to magical thinking: *If I just don't talk about it, maybe it will go away.* Having worked in human services and clinical mental health for a great portion of my professional career, I can tell you that when you peel back leaf after leaf of excessive worry, it is common to find that fear of death lies at the heart of any incapacitating anxiety. Our brains work overtime to run from death, and this can lead to sensations and feelings that seem overwhelming and can incapacitate some people altogether.

It is always fascinating to break down how some human characteristics that are so troubling today might have served the human race in its early days. It seems obvious in that historical context that the drive to stay alive was accompanied by fear of death.

Early humans faced huge risk at every turn, and failing to be hyper-vigilant could end in the decimation of a whole group of people.

Fortunately, evolution has generally decreased our need to be constantly on alert and running from accidental death or attack. Yes, those survival mechanisms will always be a part of us. We will notice an increase in our fight-flight-freeze symptoms during times when our health, safety, and wellbeing feel threatened, such as a worldwide pandemic or those times we feel there is a sudden, acute threat. It is not in the best interest of our mind-body health to spend excessive time in those states. (We will unpack that more later and discuss some simple ways to shift our physiology to an increased sense of ease.)

Dealing with our thoughts and feelings surrounding death and grief is something like dismantling an artichoke. We have to wade through the bristly, bitter, hard bits, sometimes choking on the heartbreak of it all—and nearly losing ourselves—to finally arrive at the heart of it; to be honest about what lies beneath, and what is aching and calling for attention at our tender core.

It's not a journey everyone can take with their heart and mind wide open. But you, my friend, are here to find that tender morsel in an area of our existence that for so many evokes dissonance, terror, disdain, dread, even horror: death.

Despite the pain it brings, as Zenith Virago, who calls herself a DeathWalker and has spent decades companioning people at end of life, points out in her trainings, we also experience intrigue, a desire to be close to that magic place—the threshold between life and death. We want to lightly touch that electric space enough to get a wee taste of it.

Many of us have known that place and are drawn to return, where one almost steps right into the space of dying, and what comes after, with another person. One foot in this world and one foot in the beyond.

We send off their bodily vessel into the sea of the great mystery, one foot on dry land and one on their departing boat, and at the very last minute try to pull back and have both feet resting on the solid shore. Sometimes, though, part of us seems to linger above the water, or plunges into the depths, rendering us soaked to the bone. Fully arriving back on dry land can be its own difficult transition, especially if a piece of our essence has left on the boat with our beloved one.

Of course, there are also sudden deaths that wake us in the night and render us forever dismantled by the trauma they rode in on.

Death experiences can never be fully explained or compared, because they are so very unique to each and every human. The sunflowers in a vastly planted field all appear identical, but on closer inspection are individual. Such is death and how we experience it.

Having dealt with death and dying throughout my life and career, the end of life has always held a special place of interest for me. You could say my spirit felt called to that transitional space. I have felt very much the same about birth. Even as a child, I was captivated by transitions into and out of the world's sacredness.

Throughout the years, I tried to meet the challenges of handling death head-on and in a variety of ways. Early in my career, I took time to sit with the dying when my busy nursing workload suggested that type of "compassionate care" (spoken almost with a roll of the eyes by a bristly charge nurse) was not the priority.

Within my work I tiptoed towards a change in my environment: insisting, for example, that care after death be conducted with some sacred attention; speaking with med students and doctors about their need to come to terms with their own feelings about death if they were

6

going to sit with patients as they neared the end of life, and encouraging them to look beyond defining death as a medical failure; conducting Dignity Therapy—developed and researched by Dr. Harvey Chochinov, a psychiatrist who specializes in palliative care—with dying people.

But it was my journey with my soul-connect brother during his year-long odyssey with brain cancer and ensuing death that compelled me to step up and do more to bring these conversations out of the closet. Creating and immersing myself in *The Death Dialogues Project* was, admittedly, one way I coped with my own grief. My mother, who lived with us and with whom I was very close, had a very mindful death nine months after my brother's. Then both in-laws died within the next six months. And death has continued to visit our family.

About seven months after my brother's death, I was in the early planning of staging *The Vagina Monologues* for the annual V-Day protest against violence towards women and children, when I wondered whether my deceased brother was whispering a directive in my ear.

Bec, you need to facilitate these conversations surrounding death. We need to get death out of the closet, too.

You see, American playwright Eve Ensler had interviewed 200 women about a topic we don't readily talk about: their vaginas. Then she created a renowned, award-winning piece of verbatim theatre consisting of monologues written from those interviews.

Shortly after that whisper, *The Death Dialogues Project* was born.

Interviewing people about their stories of death was always a moving experience. The tellers would express gratitude for being given the space to open their hearts and share their loved ones' stories freely. They found the experience transformational, and for many, it was the first time they'd ever told their story. Some of these experiences had occurred decades earlier.

The Death Dialogues Project led to a couple of well-received stage productions created from death stories, as well as a social media presence and a podcast developed to share these stories more broadly. Within three years after my brother's death in January 2017, we'd staged four productions, counting *The Vagina Monologues*, put together a workshop on death and created the podcast.

I like to call the project a meeting at the crossroads of social action and art.

I'd be remiss not to mention that, in the cracks between all these happenings, I was deeply grieving, missing the pillars and soul-connects of my complicated family of origin.

After some prodding, realizing that a podcast could reach a broader audience, we started *The Death Dialogues Project* podcast. It offers an opportunity for people to dismantle the myth of one-dimensional descriptions of end-of-life issues—tragic, devastating— and to get a privileged view into another person's intimate and boundless story.

Admittedly, a podcast met the *all or nothing* demands the Covid-19 pandemic dumped on our doorstep. If we could not create productions for the public to attend, we could create conversations to engage the wider world. Having received overwhelmingly positive responses from people about the impact of those conversations on their lives, the podcast seems a beautiful way to carry on the mission of drawing conversations about death and dying out of the closet.

death is not a failure

We're often fed the lie that in life, anything less than "good" is failure. And that view, my friends, deprives us of the sweetest nectar of life.

If you've listened to our podcast, you will have heard me speak of *full-spectrum living.*

In every conversation I have had with people who have experienced unimaginable loss—and walked the terrain of death with a willingness to be open to expansion— they report their lives are forever changed.

Not diminished, but expanded.

It's the beautiful-horrible of it all that comes from our stories that feel terrible-no-good.

We can feel guilty for even admitting the possibility that the death of someone we loved dearly was partly responsible for breaking us open to such an extent that we are now living in a more expansive manner. But I encourage you to give yourself that permission.

Permission to expand when your wings begin to sprout.

It may take years of walking through the hell-fires of missing your loved one so very deeply. But feeling *all* the feelings is what fertilizes the growth of your full-spectrum living.

This is a new era we are living in, when it comes to the topic of death and dying. There is a wave building of death-workers, death-talkers, death-positive allies, open-grievers—and it's changing the cultural silence surrounding death.

By sitting with open conversations, such as our chats on *The Death Dialogues Project Podcast*, you get practice at simply being still and listening to another human's deep and moving story.

Yes, in a way it's a free therapeutic intervention. Because all that people really want or need, in times of great trauma or loss, is someone who deeply understands what they are going through, at a time when it feels like no one can. Someone who can offer unconditional acceptance of wherever they are at in their process.

If we really examine the underbelly of our death-averse culture, we discover that avoidance is born of fear. And what is the frontline treatment for extreme fear or phobia?

Exposure therapy.

Simply put, experiencing that which you fear the most and learning that you are still able to breathe and function in its presence can be the cure.

Full stop.

Not that you are orgasmic about the experience, but that you can, in fact, tolerate it. That means no longer running from death, attempting to hide from it. What we do to avoid death is often like a toddler who shuts her eyes, thinking that if she can't see someone, they can't see her. Death will always see us. Why not look it in the eye?

For people who struggle to be present with difficult stories, our episodes give you an opportunity to step into that uncomfortable space at your extreme convenience. When I say that you'll be a better human for listening, I mean it. By opening yourself to conversations and stories about death, you will feel more confident in the face of the inevitable, and that will be a gift to those around you as well as yourself.

Recently, there was another whisper in my ear—to begin this writing project.

People report searching for reading material they can relate to in the immediate aftermath of death. Something that makes them feel less alone, where they can see others have lived through the deep pain they are experiencing.

People tell us they are exhausted by reading academic-type texts telling us what we *should* be experiencing, and when, how our grief may be heading towards pathology, and all sorts of clinical speculation.

They're frustrated by the bastardization of Elisabeth Kübler-Ross's famous stages of grief, created to define the emotional stages people go through after receiving diagnosis of a terminal illness. *Don't tell me my feelings are linear or have to fit that model.* Her description of five stages of grief (denial, anger, bargaining, depression, and acceptance) was actually written to explain the reactions of people who receive a terminal diagnosis, which was how it was taught to me in nursing school in the early '80s.

What people actually want, and thrive from, is hearing another person's real-life experience. We aren't fools. We know that you can't wrap up death, dying and the aftermath in a tidy container and tie it up with a bow. But when we listen to a story, bits of it are filed into places such as: *Yes, that resonates, that was similar to my experience.* Or: *I may have to call on that in the future.* Our reservoir of death literacy is generously replenished.

Many people have commented that following *The Death Dialogues Project* has informed them and made them feel more grounded as they deal with a recent death or head into watching their loved one's life winding down. That has been the payment, graciously received, for the work of this project.

Maybe you, too, are here because you are thinking: *I want to know I'm not alone, and I want to hear how others have navigated this jagged terrain.*

We are here for you.

Again, welcome.

a note on the format of the book

What you will find here are common threads that have been shared within people's stories, including my own. Each topic is one that's been discussed so frequently, you may find comfort hearing about it.

Unique individuals have unique experiences. But common threads do exist, and this book creates a beautifully-messy display out of those threads.

May the contents within these pages land gently in your heart.

We know that we learn most from shared experiences, people's stories, and we hope you find some comfort and a feeling of: *Yes, I've found a space where people get me.*

Accept this as a nourishing resource from which you can pick up and read whatever your heart is calling out for at any given time. At the end of the book, you will find a list of relevant conversations from our podcast so you can easily listen to those who have walked a similar path with loss.

The hope is that, within these pages, you find a balm to soothe your soul and a focus that centers your rambling mind. These words have been written understanding the tricks that death, loss and grief can play on our fragile brains. You will find shorter sections pertinent to a particular topic within some of the chapters.

This is not meant to be a comprehensive resource. Rather, think of it as something like an antiquated key that may unlock some of the places your weary mind has been going as you have pondered death or dealt with its aftermath.

Poems open each chapter, and they are completed with words of nourishment to ponder. Throughout, you will also find the words of contributors who generously share a glimpse of their own experience.

My wish for your experience with this book is that within these pages you will find a variety of places you may turn to as your experience of death and grief evolves within you. As our experiences change, our needs change.

Thanks for being here.

may the words here comfort and provide you with a sense of connection

may you feel your body relax and experience a deep exhale, through knowing that you are not alone

may you feel the love of those who have gone before you as you explore deeply

story

holding to tomorrow
for if dreams die
tonight will be the last

asking not of what you give
for if dreams die
the gifts will wither through

loving with abandon
for if dreams die
our hope may follow swiftly

seeing you before me
for if dreams die
the last of you will too

This project was built on the sacred ground of story.

Story was how our ancestors gathered and shared, frequently around a blazing fire.

Story, when sharing another's experience, touches on a deep, cellular level.

Story holds us gently, reminding us that we are not alone in carrying *the hard*.

Story connects us to our present and past, our fellow humans, our compassion.

Story invites our fears and difficult feelings to come out for airing.

The first interview conducted for this project was with Madeleine, whose son, Mahyan, died at six years of age. We sat at her kitchen table, recorder between us, and she spoke for two and a half hours. It felt like we could have sat there, her talking, me listening, for the rest of our lives.

After the document was transcribed, I looked at the pages of silver and gold Madeleine had shared, and I wondered how I could ever condense their story down to be part of a ninety-minute verbatim play. I still don't know the answer to that question.

I whittled and pushed and pulled. I could only get it down to twenty minutes. I read it to my husband. His face went pale. *This will change people,* he said.

Next I sat across the desk from my theater creative consultant, who kindly agreed to be there for me throughout the process. She too, wide-eyed, voiced the feeling that there was magic here, understanding my concern that it was impossible to further pare these precious words down.

That's how it was decided that this piece would be used to stage a debut of the project, introducing our community to what sitting with conversations of death felt like and the power of verbatim theatre, created using the exact words of the people interviewed.

Years ago, I had been in *The Laramie Project,* a verbatim play based on the murder of young, gay Matthew Shepard in Laramie, Wyoming. It was baptism by fire, leaving me with an understanding of the transformative power of verbatim theatre. I looked forward to what our New Zealand community would think about this offering.

So, in the name of verbatim theatre, the transcription was pulled apart like a puzzle of love and yearning and tears and damning and praise. What you will read was an attempt to reassemble and convey the beautiful-horrible of Mahyan's expansive story from the words of his gorgeous, heart-centered mama, Madeleine.

You can listen to Madeleine's episode of *The Death Dialogues Project Podcast,* Episode 97, where she not only unpacks what it was like sharing her story in such an intense way but also shares bits of Mahyan's precious story that were lost in the surgical process of disassembly and reassembly.

The verbatim piece is read on that episode as well. So many people said, as Madeleine reiterates on her podcast episode, that even with the difference of accents between us, they heard her voice in that reading. Maybe the difference actually let people hear it in a different way, where the words landed in the place that was aching to sit with them.

On our website you can read the overwhelming response from the audience. At the end, many sat down and remained in their seats, sub-grouped within their little communities, and talked and talked after the production had ended, lights up, leaning over to be closer to the words coming out of each other's mouths. Faces emoting—laughter, tears, hugs, affirmations. It was a beautiful thing to observe as it unfolded, inspired by walking for a moment in Madeleine's shoes.

During this evening of *The Death Dialogues Project* debut there were also gentle words from the celebrant at Mahyan's funeral, music from the community drop-in choir Madeleine is a part of, and words from Madeleine herself.

The beautiful and the horrible, indeed.

Love and remembrance in action.

Take some deep breaths, ground yourself, and climb into the love of this mama as she shares her dear boy within these words. Join us at the birthplace of this project.

Here are Madeleine's words about Mahyan, who was six years old at the time of his death. He had a brain tumor in the left frontal lobe.

The spaces to share are not present in a lot of our lives.

Just over a year ago I spoke at a child cancer memorial day. And for me it was the first time in the 14 years after Mahyan died—*that* was the first time someone had ever *asked* me to share about his death.

He died not quite two years after his diagnosis.

At the time of diagnosis, it was the absolute last thing on my mind.

It was not even in my reality—and they said, "It's serious, he needs to be in Starship (children's hospital), tomorrow." And *that* I feel my body still holds the shock and trauma of—that initial diagnosis to come out of nowhere.

So he had surgery to remove it, and there were two oncologists. The radiologist offered radiotherapy, and the oncologist said if you don't do radiotherapy he will die.

So when they said to us, "This is how he'll survive it," it

didn't add up to what we'd found for ourselves, so I went back and said, "Show me, tell me—where is the research?"

And they couldn't. They said, "This is what we can offer you, and you are within your rights not to do this."

So we started to go ahead with radiation and did all the preparation, and then my gut said: *This is not what we are supposed to be doing.*

We pretty much said, "Let us take him home."

The biggest shift for me has been stepping into the *yes/and,* not the *either/or.*

That's what that did for me, because I saw that I would do *anything* if I felt that was his chance to live, and at the same time I felt like it had to be in nourishment. It had to be in alignment with how he was born, how he was fed, how he'd been raised, how he'd been parented.

So he did have surgery, and they said if we didn't do radiation, they could just help support us to keep him as comfortable as possible.

And we were out of the hospital system.

He knew he was sick, but I wasn't familiar or didn't have a lot of skill around it, so I don't feel like we had a lot of open conversations around that.

My mum remembers—he was really adventurous—and my mum said something like, "Ah, you almost gave me a heart attack doing that," and he said, "Ah, don't worry, I have another two years left."

We have memories of his wisdom around that.

I remember sitting on his floor and I said, "I wanna have a talk about where we go," and Mahyan cut me off and said, "Look, Mum, I'm going home, I know I'm going home."

He hadn't heard that from me. He was very clear that he was going home. And that was as much as he wanted to talk about it.

I remember him being in his bed.

And then I remember singing, you know, "Bob The Builder?"

We used to sing Bob the Farter. And I treasure that.

You have this incredible decompensation and then, there you are singing, "Bob The Farter, can you smell it? Yes we can!"

Interestingly, he was really unwell; he has the surgery; then he had this incredible year.

He was homeschooling. He was fit and healthy. You could have never known.

He was swimming. He was active. He had no illness. None. We were thinking: cured.

He was so healthy.

But he did become unwell after about ten months.

We went back to Starship and I said: Look. They did a scan and they said, "Yes, it's back and it's big."

The surgeon—who I loved— is walking down the hall, and he wasn't going to be shown the scans, but he said, 'Let me do it again."

He did the surgery again.

He was in recovery for less than a week; then we were back up here.

On the way home, we stopped at Ruakaka Beach. Beautiful day but no one is swimming. Here he is with a fresh scar, but he's been given the okay to swim. *Where is everyone?* No one's on the beach. He didn't care, he went in and had this beautiful swim, and then someone came down and said, "Ah, there's been a shark sighting." Everyone cleared out.

So here's this boy on his way back from having major brain surgery, straight to swimming with a shark.

Mahyan wasn't quite right and just not bouncing back the way he'd previously done.

Then his sixth birthday was in April. And he was not well. Things are looking not so great. But for his birthday, it was bizarre. He was really, really well. He had from May to October then, being really well. Happy, healthy. Yeah.

And we went on this little holiday to the snow, and while we were there, he started wetting the bed. Or then he'd look up and be saying, "I can't see it, what are you looking at?"

And we were going, oh, can he see, can he see, is he not able to see? And then he slowly lost his sight over the next few weeks.

This was really important to me: I think I'm usually Miss Positivity, and it's taken me a long time to be okay with the darkness and the darker parts of life, and I remember he got out of the bed and he walked down the hallway and smacked into the doorframe because he couldn't see, and I'm holding him.

He was crying and upset, and I'm saying, "It's all right, it's all right," and he yells at me, "CAN'T YOU SEE IT'S NOT ALL RIGHT?"

And yeah, and it changed something for me, and I was then: *You're right, it's not all right.*

And we just sat there then. And at the same time, I feel that he then had a real freedom from that point.

And it was like, goodness, this feels really beautiful, in that somehow, with losing his sight, he just felt incredibly free.

I remember the funeral. I had a 12-day-old baby strapped to my chest who was singing, which was part of the most beautiful memories that I had.

There was five days between Isaac being born and Mahyan dying.

That has been the single most powerful thing, because he was born at home and Mahyan died at home, and they— I feel really goose-bumpy saying it now—the feeling was the same.

Incredibly the same.

And I had never, ever been around anyone that had died

20

before. No grandparents. No one.

Sometimes it was a blessing that I had never done death, because all I had was how I'd done birth to go by.

So when people offered to give us respite in hospice we said, "Can someone come to us?" And they said, "Yes."

Our hospice nurse had known Mahyan.

That feeling of being held.

We were held by people that loved us, even in a professional capacity.

So that is beautiful. And I'm incredibly grateful. And I didn't know it was different to what could have been.

Having home births is the time that I have felt closest to the Divine.

That is in that otherworldly space—and I also had an experience while Isaac was being born, of seeing Mahyan in that space.

And I remember that my midwife came and said, "It's okay, hon, it's just transition." She heard things change for me and I'm crying and she's saying, "It's okay, hon, you're nearly there," and I'm like going, "It's not the birth! It's not the birth."

Because Mahyan was, like, in my bedroom—two doors down—in my bedroom with my mum snuggled up with him, and we had *never* given up hope. We were still trying new things.

And when he was in that space—of when I was in labor—*that* was the first time I knew that if he was *there* he wasn't going to stay *here*.

It was confirmation to me.

It was the most incredible feeling of *there was a baby born*, and we took him into the bed and did everything with him right alongside Mahyan.

And Mahyan, he was kind of awake; he didn't have much energy at all.

He can't see.

He was able to hold Isaac and feel him and smile at that.

21

And that was the last coherent thing he did.

He went into a coma that night of Isaac's birth.

And we just stayed in that space.

Interestingly, the day he died, I was sitting in the bed feeding the baby and Mahyan's next to me and there's this song in my head—*I'm Saying Goodbye to You.*

And I was totally in denial—I was like, *Why is this song in my head? Why is this song in my head? Get out of my head.*

And then—that was the day—he died and I'm like: *Aww babe, I should have taken that opportunity for a conversation or to just share.*

Mahyan was in a coma and had a nasal gastric tube.

That was one of the things we fought for, I guess.

We had hope … and colostrum and breast milk that could be put in there.

That's incredible to me, that his last food was his first food.

We had a couch that pulled out into a bed and we were in the lounge and just holding him, and I remember we all were sharing and talking, memories. But it is singing that most stands out in my memory. Songs we had sung as lullabies, childhood favorites. Anything to get us through—and then we could see that his breathing was getting further apart.

For the most part it was very beautiful.

We felt that he'd maybe taken his last breath and—without notice—up the steps walked his doctor, and he took his pulse and it was gone.

I remember that night being very precious.

And I remember Joel coming over from across the road and coming in and saying to everyone, "Ah come on, cheer up."

He's four years old.

"What's going on? Cheer up. What are you all looking so sad about?"

22

I think the moment for Joel didn't come until the funeral.

One of my husband's best friends took me to the funeral, and Joel on the way said, "This means I'm not going to see him again."

And interestingly, that stays with me, because Joel, like me, like we all do, we all have some level of post-traumatic stress that we live with.

I remember that first night snuggling into bed, Mahyan just stayed in my bed.

He died at sunset, and we put him in my bed.

I think someone had called and talked to my husband about using cotton wool and keeping him cool, and I think it triggered the thought … I had the thought: *Oh my, how bad is this going to be?*

We had a family friend who was an undertaker, so—they brought him to have him embalmed.

And they brought him back.

And he stunk. Like Pine O Clean.

And I can't ever … that's my one thing that I go … everything else was an incredible experience, but if I had known that they would bring my son back to me smelling like disinfectant and toilet cleaner, I would never have let him go.

But I didn't know. No one talks about that.

I had a new baby—Isaac slept in my arms on this side and Mahyan was on that side for that first night, and then it was the next day they took him north.

I remember music, and an odd person coming while I was just with my two little ones, and he came back in his favorite orange shirt and we put some hair in the casket too, because he was a hair twirler; he'd snuggle up and twirl hair.

We kept him then in my room, and I have the memory of Joel driving his car around the edge of the casket—just playing—and it just made it: *This is what happens, this is how it should be.*

23

So the midwife—a *beautiful* gatekeeper; she's Maori—she comes to check on me while Mahyan's body was up north, the next day after he died, and she comes to the door ... *and the wailing.*

It was so beautiful.

She cried, she wailed, and brought this noise, this incredible experience, into us sitting there going: *Fuck, what just happened?* It was so uncomfortable and so incredible at the same time.

And then at the funeral ... and then she karangaed us onto the grounds at the funeral.

And remembering there was also this incredible distraction of this brand-new baby.

So some people just came and held the baby. I remember someone just sitting on my chair with the baby just laying on her chest. So there was a positive—just life and death—right there.

And he was a baby with no name—because who can be naming a baby during this? In the newspaper, it is everyone else's name ... "and baby." That was a distraction, everyone wondering what we were going to name him.

The time between his death and funeral got us used to— I feel because I had such an experience of that palpable other-worldliness—from that birth and that night of him dying, that when his body came back from the embalmers, it did not feel like it was Mahyan, it didn't.

It was like—here's your body.

And that was a gift. That was a *real* gift, that we had the experience of having him there long enough.

I don't feel like I really expected anyone to ever know what to say.

"This is hard." To just say: *This is hard.* But their actions, even if their actions say, *it's too hard to come*—I totally get that.

My earlier experience around that was people said,

24

"Have you talked to him about death?" And I said, "Kind of," but I was in a lot of denial and a part of me was like: *What do you mean, death. How dare you?* And the only time I really got angry was with a woman who had lost a child in a similar way and her words—she came in when Mahyan was quite unwell—and her words were, "I'm so pleased I've seen him before he died."

I was angry because she had spoken it.

I was like: *You are not allowed to speak that out loud.*

It's almost like living two parallels.

We were doing everything we could for him to live longer with us. And everything I had read, trusted in, prayed about, gave me trust in what would happen.

Again, it's a: Yes he will live *and* he may die. Not, yes he will live and no he won't die.

Maybe it was just that until he died, it was a bit like the diagnosis; it was not in my head. What confirms that for me was that I did nothing to plan a funeral.

So the people around me said, "Let's make this about Mahyan—and what does that look like?"

I was really clear I wanted the funeral outside. People were standing. We had a silk scarf rainbow over his casket. His friends put stickers all over the casket.

The thing that was really hard was, people wanted to speak and we had a timeframe to get him to cremation, which never really felt right for me.

I did end up feeling that it didn't really matter as much, because it wasn't really him anymore anyway.

I've never done anything with his ashes.

Yeah, but at the actual funeral there was a beautiful meditation of seeing him on his magic carpet and offering to send up a color for him.

If I hadn't had so many miracles and so much love, and like, experiential love about the whole thing, there's no way I could have done this. In fact, I don't know if I've done it particularly well—and one of the hardest things to hear people say in those early days (whispers), "You're doing so well."

THIS? THIS is what "well" feels like?

Yes, I've felt him.

The first one comes to mind is a dream not long after he died, and he danced with me. He was standing on my toes.

And it was different because I woke up going: *That wasn't a dream.*

And there were only a couple of those.

I had this dream and he just walked up the back yard. He was strong and healthy and a young man and was like, "Mum, I'm fine. I'm so fine."

That was not a dream.

About five years ago I ended up with a stomach ulcer and was very, very unwell.

That experience—a conflict—something happened that broke everything. I was turning forty and my people wouldn't be there, and I ended up being so very unwell.

I didn't know at the time I had a stomach ulcer. I felt like I was having some kind of nervous breakdown. I could not stop crying, and my body was shaking, in shock.

I cried for three days and nights. I couldn't sleep. I had massive insomnia.

And on the third night, I heard Mahyan start talking to me.

He spent the next three days and nights with me. Just talking and sharing and answering questions. Just being there.

That was a truth, and it changed my life forever.

He showed me how loved I was, and how it felt to be totally loving.

During this space I could ask him anything.

It was sporadic. And then slowly, over time, that finished, but the feeling and experience of it never finished, and *that* changed my grief experience.

It was so massive for me.

I think it was *totally* Mahyan.

I was given the role and shown that I am a gate-keeper—someone that has the calling of birth and death.

Another one, I was given the name "Stitches."

I thought: *What the heck?*

Then last year I read this wonderful book on a thousand ways to listen, where it talked about—and I've always felt really called in that work of—how do we hear each other. Maybe some of that for me comes from me not being comfortable to ask questions. And I think of that with Mahyan's journey. And in that book it talked about stitches, and stitches are how we listen; we are stitching the worlds together, and that is something for me—is that we are bringing the heavens and earth and the divine and the human together.

I had no clue why I was given that word, and then reading that, it all made sense.

I went to my doctor about the experience, and she said, "Wow. This is really okay."

Holding space for each other's different grieving is really, really hard.

It's been important to hold space for things to be known and unknown. For there to be mystery and information.

Synchronicity has *really* helped me walk along the hard and the shit and the sorrow and pulls me a little bit back to trust.

You can trust this.

This is hard *and* you can trust this.

This is horrid *and* you can trust this.

This is hideous *and* you can trust this.

Yes, and gratitude and joy can coexist with rage and sorrow and shadow.

Embracing that brokenness, too, is actually seeing that. I think for a long time I wanted to be fixed. Like, I didn't expect that I would ever get through grief, but I wanted to be fixed because I was broken.

Whereas the last few years are about embracing the broken. I feel like I had an openness to do grief, to do what it was going to ask of me. And I didn't realize what that physically meant. It was a separate learning.

When Mahyan came back, it healed the spiritual, perhaps, the mystery, and it's been my work, with the help of people, to uncover what it looks like to show up kindly to a body that has been broken by grief.

I do sometimes go back to: *My body wouldn't totally be crapped out if I had grieved well.* Or if I had paid attention, or healed, or ... when the truth is, who gets through this lightly?

Who gets through this and feels ... (huge inhale) yeah.

There's an expectation to be "moving through" death and grief.

Part of that is the collective invisibility of death and of talking about people who live with loss.

These things change us on a cellular level.

This is about that visibility. We've kept these things in the shadows. We need to bring it *out* of the shadows.

As time has gone by, I want to say it's okay to talk about him. Just say his name. I love hearing his name.

may you open to the listening of story, from the beautiful, to the horrible, with heart and mind wide open

may you feel the connection between us all as the words caress you

may compassion be the salve for the hurt that arises when another's story touches you deeply or breaks open a wound you have been holding close

death as a dirty word

hey you
with your head down
blinders on to avoid
death's gaze
i see you
i understand you
no judging you for
your inability to be
mired in others' loss
go on pretending
death is not a thing
dance with your fleeting
innocence while you are able
until
death knocks on your door
bringing you over to
our side of town
in the meantime
just love us
just be there
we know you will be joining us
it's okay if you don't

I was immersed in death from an early age. What was modeled for me was more about showing up in the ceremonial spaces, not so much about showing up emotionally for others in the weary fields of *before* or the expanse of the *after*: the most important work of death.

My mother, who was born in 1922, talked frequently about experiences surrounding death. A daughter of sharecroppers, she spoke of how, in the dust bowl of Oklahoma, death care was handled within the home, much like births.

There was the story of little Billy, who came to live with my mother's family when his mother died. My mother was the youngest of her family and he was younger still, arriving as a toddler. Billy was what they called a *blue baby*, caused by a heart defect that gave the skin a blue tint due to the lack of adequate oxygenation. He died at an early age, which left a deep impression on my mother. As a child, I would ask her to tell me the story over and over again.

A common theme in her stories of death and birth was the children being sent *up yonder,* to a big boulder that sat high on the property they lived on, as far away from the house as possible, so as not to bear witness to the actual events. She recalled her sister on top of the big boulder, hands on hips, belting out the hymn: *On Christ the solid rock I stand, all other ground is sinking sand* ... .

Clearly, these transitional events made a lasting impression, even when the child was protected from seeing the grit of what was occurring.

Return from *up yonder* and what will you find? A life added or a life taken away.

There was one story my mother told me of her young adult years that impressed me deeply, on so many levels, and has remained etched in my heart.

When my parents were young, they and another couple shared a wall in the duplex they lived in. There was a connecting door, and much of their time was spent sharing the labor of parenting, cooking meals together, and socializing. This would have been in the 1940s. The neighbor couple had a toddler who required a daily dose of medicine. The mother would put a tablet in jam, thinking this made it easier to swallow.

One day, my mother's friend, having trouble getting the wee one to swallow, tried to assist the process and the pill became lodged in the child's airway. She ran to my mother, who took the toddler into her arms. They held the child upside down, banging on the toddler's back and doing all things imaginable to attempt to dislodge the pill. Desperate, they ran to the doctor's home nearby, where he attempted to save the toddler, but it was too late. In my mother's words, 'the child died in my arms."

This is such a tragic tale. It's not easy to hear or easy to tell, but what I've shared, thus far, is not the most difficult part.

A phone call must have been made to some extended family, the husbands having joined them at the doctor's office. The doctor was a dear personal friend of all of them. They had their time of shock together and then both couples must have carried the sweet toddler to the funeral home straight away; just a few hours would have passed before they were back in the family home.

By the time they walked in the door, every trace of the precious child had been erased. Not a framed picture remained. Belongings and treasured playthings—gone. My mother's knees buckled at the sight of it. The child's name was never spoken of again, as if the child had never existed.

Wiping away every trace of this sweet child's existence is the saddest part of this story, to me. And sadder still is knowing that we were born from stories such as these, where death was ignored and therefore a legacy of a well-lived life was negated—of these things we do not speak.

This is a tragic example, and I wish I could say it's the only time I've heard such a story, but it is not. No matter what the framework through which we have learned of death or witnessed death, it's difficult for most people I've spoken with to even imagine that type of response to death in this day and age. Yet a variation on this theme continues in many families.

People have shared that they were totally kept away from death as children, even deaths of pets or farm animals. Fictions were created to explain the disappearance of these beings from their lives. Many report being kept home and not allowed to attend funerals of close relatives.

My husband is British and has never been shy about reminding me of being raised within a culture that had an inherent rule of *stiff upper lip*. Many colonized countries retain echoes of that mentality. He saw remnants of it in the United States and in New Zealand. Sometimes this was obnoxiously overt, and other times the *get on with it, hold your head up* messages were a bit more subtle.

There are repeated messages of *shouldn't you be moving on?* and people frequently feel shamed when they share their grief out loud.

These words aren't said out of compassion, to provide comfort. Subconsciously, those words are a self-centered message—*Your grief is making me very uncomfortable and I don't know how to be around it or you. Can you stop now and get back to the way you were?*

The second part of that sentence is, *because I don't think I can continue to be around you like this.* And as we will talk about later, all too often, our people do not stick around.

It's helpful to observe these serious flaws in how people communicate about, handle (or ignore) death through a lens of compassion. One night, on the heels of watching a World War II-era movie, *Jojo's Rabbit*, with our son, I tried with my husband to unpack that stiff-upper-lip mentality and its denial of death.

Suddenly, in watching the film, I had been able to imagine myself in that time as a woman, as a mother, as a deep feeler, and what it would be like to know that civilians, neighbors, were being bombed and killed—and that you and your loved ones could be a target as well. Never mind trying to erase it from your mind, with all the air-raid warnings and safety drills.

I realized, had I lived in that space, if I had let myself take on every story of death or feel every deep feeling surrounding that absolute onslaught of terror, I would have been rendered incapacitated—unable to care for myself or my family.

Not only were they face to face with stories of people they knew—families, youngsters gone off to war, schools being bombed, civilians dying en masse— but there was nowhere to hide. Of course you had to stiff-upper-lip it. Your survival depended on it.

Problem was, with so many traumatized grandparents and parents, this trait was never programmed out of the culture, and people are still made to feel less-than if they are anything but stoic. *Just get on with it; stop whining; you need to move on.*

The Death Dialogues Project is here to tell you that those messages are bullshit. We have a chance to break the pain of this generational trauma by changing our narratives about death and dying. The first step being: start talking about it.

Death deserves its rightful place within the experiences of meaningful life transitions, to be talked about, honored, grieved openly, and cherished with an understanding that your feelings for your loved one need never be buried.

Sometimes we read and hear overcorrections of the language used in terms of death—*don't say loss, it's death; don't say sleeping, it's misleading; don't say passed away* ... .

But focusing too much on what people should or shouldn't say distracts us from the tougher emotional conversations that lie beneath the surface. I don't care what you call the cause of your grief. I just want to hear your story.

Hold on to the stories you witness of cultures and people who honor death in a way that makes you feel: *Yes, my bones know this.*

When I was grieving that my significant boyfriend left and headed back to the UK, my mother shared this story suggesting I need not dwell on the loss: My mother was told, by her father, she could have two days to mourn her beloved's death by plane crash. Then she had to get on with her life. — K.B.

may we understand that the colonial over-culture has dismantled many of the organic ways of living, and that literacy about death, dying and the aftermath is one of them

may we forgive ourselves for the times we did not show up for others in a way we feel at peace with

may we walk forward committed to being open to the depths of living that the end of life can bring

anticipatory grief:
missing you while you're
still here

don't call him home yet

begging another season
for this man to walk the earth
please add more time to his life-clock
for him to love and give and receive
let no fear hover above or envelop him
but a peace in the knowing
that all we are
will always be
those left behind
would be the sufferers
to lose the love, the compassion,
the knowing shelter
where we seek solace
to feel a heart-hurt
like this is awe-full
leaving one awe-struck
all in the same
that one's passing
on from this world
might leave a gap
that had long been
stitched together
by his compassion
shared with those who have had
the honor to pass his way
it's in his suffering
i realize he grew
me from a sprout
he corrected ignorance
and planted compassion
he corrected complacence
and grew action
he saved me like no father had
and like no brother
the world has ever known

G rieving deeply for people before they die is a thing.
        If you recognize that this is a space you are in now, stop right here, let yourself exhale and sit with this knowing.

You are not alone. In this moment, other people are also mourning their loved one who is still alive.

Anticipatory grief is not morbid or something to be ignored. Sometimes we see anticipatory grief accentuated in situations of prolonged illnesses, such as ALS/motor neuron disease, cancers, Alzheimer's/dementia, advanced age, or any situation where a less than positive prognosis has been given.

Sometimes we see waves of anticipatory grief when we love people who engage in risky behaviors, as we fear for their safety.

Hearing of untimely deaths can sometimes send a surge of anticipatory grief and worry: *If it could happen to them, it could happen to anyone.* Even a heart full of deep love can bring bouts of: *What would I do if I lose this person?*

My friend Kate's father had been diagnosed with a type of leukemia when I met her. Throughout that time, she would report in on Dad, and much of the time his status was one of barely knowing he was ill. But in the last year there had been a change in her reports.

"I have a feeling Dad is winding down," she might say.

She noticed incremental changes during her visits with him every couple of months, like a snake slowly shedding its skin, until the last few months of his life, when she began openly and more frequently expressing her thoughts about his dying to me.

Kate is a person who practices emotional literacy surrounding death and dying and had been one of our storytellers in a production, sharing the story of her best friend, who had died of cancer. She knew what anticipatory grief felt like and was open to processing hers as her father's health declined.

During my brother's year of brain cancer, I admit that we were wrapped in hope, refusing to believe anything less than that this vibrant man would survive—*and* always in the back of my mind, I understood the gravity of his illness.

It was heartbreaking that the rock of our family was having to have his life altered to such a great degree, but there was always hope that the treatment would finally kick in, meaningfully, and end the nightmare. There was mourning throughout his illness.

It wasn't until my second-to-last visit with him, just a month before he died, that I sensed that the change in him wasn't because of the new chemotherapy finally giving him some side effects. I hoped upon hope that it was, but anticipatory grief hit my heart in a dramatic fashion. There was less than a month until his death to sit with the fact that this disease process might not be turning around; that his brain cancer seemed to be advancing.

We no longer had the opportunity for the long talks we had prior to his illness, about life and death. Although lucid right in the moment, his short-term memory had taken leave, due to the area of his brain affected, and I know the entire family grieved that part of him during the year of his illness.

The marathon phone calls didn't come.

He was no longer able to hold our concerns, to share his, or to comfort so many, as he had always done. Tenderly emotional to anything touching, he teared up easily, and we struggled with how much to share any trying news with him.

Every time he was reminded of a death in our family he would

40

cry, as if it was the first time he heard it. On a road trip during his illness I played The Band and he asked, "How's Levon Helm doing?" When I told him he'd died a while back—which he'd previously known—he sobbed.

So yes, anticipatory grief can come in all shapes and sizes, and in reaction to a variety of happenings within the space of illness, or life itself.

After my brother died, which tore my heart out, my mother, who lived with us, started a more rapid trajectory towards death within her 95th year. (She died nine months later.)

Ever alert and eloquent, she went through a variety of stages in processing her upcoming death. Like Kate, she was very open and literate about death, especially in this stage of her life, when so many of her friends had gone before her. The need to dive deep into her impending death arose after her son's illness and death, something she felt a parent should never have to witness.

My brother, my rock, my best friend, my confidant, with whom I processed the entirety of our upbringing, had left the planet. At the same time, my mother was vocally coming to terms with her end of life.

At once it hit me that this terrain I was heading into, this life stage, was one my brother and I had always imagined traveling together. We would support each other during our mother's end of life. But when I impulsively went to call him or to email him, the reality was gut-wrenching. My precious backup was no longer at the other end of the telephone line, and this was my journey to walk with my mother.

Insult to injury, indeed.

Witnessing my mother process her life, including choices made during our traumatic childhoods that she was less than proud of—all in the midst of imagining what life could be like without either of my lifelong supports—could easily bring me to my knees.

I've heard tell of soul-connects you have on the other side, that you make contracts with about life together before you are born. If that's true, they're mine.

Thank heaven for them. They were my life raft.

My mother and I talked during those months between my brother's death and hers. Or, I should say, she mainly talked and I listened. If she had a bad cold or felt unwell, she'd say to my brother, "Hold open the door, I'm coming through."

She grieved the life she didn't have: the security she wasn't able to give her children, the true love she'd turned her back on earlier, who certainly would have been a kinder and gentler husband.

As she shared her remorse and regrets, I, just off the odyssey of brain cancer with my dear brother, frequently sat shell-shocked, feeling gutted while also nodding, wanting her to feel heard and validated. Repeating the mantra, "Mom, you did the best you could under the circumstances."

Mind you, I also frequently retreated to my room.

Her processing made me admit that I could not always step into the 24/7 helper role. My grief was still having its way with me. The things she needed to process would bring up hurts my brother and I had shared and processed throughout our lives. The energy just wasn't there to sort through it all again and endure the emotional fallout.

At times I wanted to scream, "Take me out of this fucked-up movie!" while simultaneously dreading the end of her story, knowing she was telling stories I wanted permanently etched on my heart.

I did not want to lose another life-long companion, my precious mother and best friend. I did not want to be, of the three of us, the last one standing.

Based on stories shared with me, there seem to be common threads within anticipatory grief that can feel very confusing. Sometimes there is a curiosity, a deep desire to know the answer to *when:*

How much longer do you think they have?

How long will this go on?

What will their death look like?

In some situations, especially during prolonged illness or visible

42

suffering, there may be a hidden desire for their person to die, and this frequently heralds much guilt. Maybe it helps to understand that it may not be that you wish the death of someone as much as you wish an end to their suffering.

If we are being honest, consider that caretaking can be exhausting and overwhelming. It's very human to feel wisps of: *I need this to stop.*

These can be normal reactions to extraordinary circumstances, and it's important to give yourself grace and understanding.

My mother lived with us during her last two years of life. In hindsight, my husband and I (both previously medical professionals) have discussed how fearful we were that she might fall and break a hip or have a stroke. We were afraid of something happening to her that might render her bedridden and suffering from pain and a very limited quality of life.

My initial adult work with humans was in nursing homes, and I had seen, up close, how people who appeared to be on death's door could linger for years, bodies stiff and contracted, depressed, sometimes unable to communicate.

Of course, no one wishes that for their loved ones' final journey, but sometimes we know too much, and, in hindsight, that possibility frightened us more than we realized at the time.

We went to extremes of assuring her safety as much as we could, absolutely in prevention mode. If only we'd known how graceful her exit would be, we could have exhaled, and our time would have felt a bit lighter in her final months.

Before my mother died, I was heading off to a silent retreat for self-care. She insisted I go because I'd canceled a previous one when she had a cold virus. We knew she was waiting for the train to take her "home," as she said, but it seemed maybe months away. She and family insisted I go.

Just in case she took a turn, I went to a medical store to pick up some supplies for my husband. I shared my mother's status with the woman who checked me out. And let me be frank: if it hadn't been for my mother's open narration, we'd have had no idea where she was in her winding-down process, based on how she presented physically.

The staff person informed me that the previous week she had sat with her best friend as she died. She instructed me: *Ask your team and her angels to gather around her and make this process as gentle as possible.*

During the starlit nights at the retreat, in the far north of New Zealand, where the sky feels like you can reach out and touch the vastness of the heavens, I would look up and beckon my brother and all of the teams that might be swirling beyond or within galaxies to rally themselves and take their places. I was going to need their strength and support to serve my mother well on her journey.

At times I had participated in the care of my brother, throughout his illness, and during his last week of life. It was my highest honor to do so, but I cannot tell you the amount of dread I had for doing the same for my mother. Mind you, I wouldn't have had it any other way.

You can sense the beautiful-horrible-messiness swirling within me, can't you?

I wanted to serve in that ultimate caregiving capacity, and she had asked it of me after hearing the beauty of my brother's experience at his time of dying and in the aftermath of his death.

Simply, I was still hurting so badly and, having been at the bedside of death many times, I knew that it was impossible to predict what type of transition would take place. I ached at my very core at the thought of witnessing my sweet mother suffering. Utter dread.

Those teams must have rallied on the other side, but I wasn't expecting such a rapid response. The moment I returned from the retreat, my mother looked at me as she sat on the edge of the bed, and said, "This is it, Becky, I'm dying now. I'm going to go."

And twenty-four hours later, she'd taken her miraculous flight. But that's another story.

Different health and wellbeing conditions bring different time-lines and a variety of emotional responses.

With Alzheimer's dementia, people speak of watching their

loved one slowly losing parts of themselves—their cognition, their personality, their functioning—like autumn leaves gradually wafting away from the life force of the tree. There's no rational order, and it can be a torturous journey for family to witness their loved one's essence fade, morphing into someone so far removed from their previous selves.

People dealing with degenerative illnesses may have a slow decline and gradual loss of abilities, but frequently cognition remains intact, which can be a definition of the beautiful-horrible for them and their loved ones—remaining a companion to one whose body is fading away. Frequently the impact of that journey isn't registered while adrenaline and hyper-vigilance are in the driver's seat, but becomes more clear after the person's death.

Cancer patients may have a rapid or slow trajectory, but one thing rings universal: the grief reaction begins at the moment of diagnosis, similar to the aforementioned conditions. Remember that the five stages of grief Elisabeth Kübler-Ross defined actually originated in reference to the reaction to a cancer or other terminal illness diagnosis.

The dance begins—of treatment, or none, and if treatment is taken, which symptoms are side effects of the treatment and which of the disease, the speculation of the unfolding of the disease process. Nothing is ever clear-cut.

Maybe you have a child born differently-abled and you grieve for what you see as the hardships they may face as they go through life, or you have concern about their longevity. Maybe you've had a family member who has survived a stroke or an accident or other event and is affected in a way that renders them forever changed.

Maybe you know someone like the art professor I took care of, who, recovering well from heart surgery, was fine one minute, and then found face-down in his plate of food the next, experiencing so much oxygen deprivation that he was left in an unresponsive state.

Let us pause for a moment and consider the unseen subculture of people who live their lives in nursing homes or rehab facilities due to an accident or traumatic illness and are decades younger than the typical resident.

But let us also consider the aged residents, some of whom have no family, no visitors and feel put out to pasture, biding time until their deaths.

There are so very many stories where anticipatory grief lives.

Even in the eyes of the 20-year-old looking at their 50-year-old healthy parent and knowing that, one day, death will enter their storyline.

You might come to think: *No wonder we live in a state of death-denial; it's so sad.*

What I know for sure, based on my own experiences and the stories I've been told, is that there is no getting around *sad*. But if you can open yourself and commit to feeling the big feelings and let yourself become emotionally literate about death, dying and the aftermath, an indescribable amount of personal expansion awaits you.

With our capacity to feel the depths of grief and sadness, we gain a capacity to feel even greater joy.

It might feel slow coming, because, make no mistake about it, the aftermath of death and grief will have its way with you. But when you consciously feel *all* the feelings, they are much less likely to come out in anger or illness or substance and alcohol abuse, or any of the long list of other less-than-functional ways unclaimed grief can manifest. One day, you may notice a more heightened sense of positive emotions than ever before.

may we recognize when anticipatory grief arises in our lives, honoring it and the love we have for the person we are grieving
may we compassionately remember those who are the silent suffering, hidden away from society
may we rest easier in the awareness of the unpredictability of death's arrival

going there: the tough talks
about death

may i sit with you
and learn how it is
you want to die
may grace hold us gently
loving you into the beyond
may your truth flow freely
gently caressing all that you are
and ever more will be

There is no exact way to approach the topic of planning for dying and death with a loved one. You will be more fluent and it will be most helpful if you've already had these conversations with yourself and gotten your own thoughts and plans in order, but we know this isn't the case for most people.

One thing most of us forget when mulling how to start a challenging conversation is that one of the best ways to facilitate openness is by starting with a question.

We then need to listen closely to the other's responses and be mindful of any questions they ask. Sometimes it can be helpful to answer an inquiry regarding their thoughts before taking off with explanations.

Remember the story of parents graphically responding to their inquisitive young child's question about where babies come from, going off on a detailed tangent. The stunned child responds, "I just wanted to know if they were from New York."

Yes, that.

Sometimes, our anxiety takes the steering wheel and we forge a path into an important topic in a way that actually feels too complex for the person to absorb.

A gentle opener such as: *I understand many people shy away from conversations about our dying and death, but I just want you to know I'm ready to go there with you, if you choose.*

Have you had thoughts about any guidance you'd like to give for when life is on the decline, or at the time of your death and after your death?

It's certainly meaningful and important to be able to respect your end-of-life wishes. Would you like for me to write any down for you?

Many people will respond with minimal feedback: *I'm happy with whatever my loved ones decide for me.*

While that type of response may not be what you are hoping for, it has opened the door for further conversation if the person so chooses.

You'd think, with my experiences of death, I would have a detailed map outlining how to proceed when my dying time comes.

Yes, I have ideas and guidelines.

Yes, I have a playlist of songs; a final song to dance me out on.

Yes, I have a natural handwoven willow coffin sitting in my living room, with the understanding of whoever goes first, my partner or myself, resting in the local natural burial ground.

I have a file of thoughts surrounding my death, a living will, and last will and testament, because I know how supportive and caring those acts are for surviving loved ones. But I also understand how people can feel that the post-death time is for the living. I do desire for them to handle my body and formalities how they see fit, given the circumstances they find themselves in.

Ultimately, I want my loved ones not to feel guilt if there is something within my wishes they are unable to attend to—practically or emotionally. From the depths of my heart, I long for my loved ones to do whatever creates less stress for them and makes their heart sing.

That said, time after time, survivors say how comforted they were that their deceased loved one had left guidance and instructions for them to carry out after death. They felt it was as if their loved one was supporting them from the beyond. They felt their care, their love and a palpable sense of connection as they experienced what their departed person had created.

Beyond that, planning for one's death is a benevolent act that provides support for your survivors amid the emotional chaos and brain-fog they may experience afterward.

Grief-brain is a real thing. Knowing you are fulfilling your loved one's wishes can provide great assistance and support.

Conversely, I've heard many stories where there wasn't the slightest trail, not even breadcrumbs, leading survivors to wills, or estate plans, or any directives. I've seen and heard the anguish of folks being pushed, in the throes of grief, to go hunting through files and documents—many times to no avail, which precipitates lengthy court proceedings. Instead of allowing people to be with their emotions and attend to their loved one's farewell, this lack of preparation forces survivors to become overextended and frustrated.

Think about the comfort you could provide from beyond your death if you leave instructions.

My husband, who handles most of our business and finances, keeps a file. Every time before he travels, he sits me down and reminds me where I will find what I need and who the professionals are that will help guide me if he dies before me. That doesn't feel morbid. It feels smart and kind; an act of service that comes from his love for his family.

Maybe sharing knowledge of similar experiences and how it can be such a gift to the survivors will open the door a bit for your person to consider conducting some of their own planning.

And never forget, role modeling is the most effective method of teaching. Take care of your own end-of-life business and speak openly of it.

Jane Cunningham created a lovely, free online guide for facilitating conversations surrounding the end of life. I've used it and have heard from others who have and found it extremely helpful. You can find it at www.gentle-conversations.com

Most medical establishments have normalized conversations about advance directives. An advance directive is a statement signed by a person that sets out, in advance, treatment wanted or not wanted, in the event they become unwell in the future. This type of document can sometimes be referred to as a living will, and there are common-alities between them. Look into how you can obtain such a document to complete.

In the US, before every medical appointment, there was a check-in about whether I'd completed mine.

The New Zealand government has a comprehensive advance directive document that can be completed and filed with your general practitioner. Our living will is at our attorney's office, with our other will and end-of-life documentation.

Wills, end-of-life planning, and advance directives aren't scary. They are smart. The website caring.com says that while less than 25% of people surveyed have a will, 60% say that they think having a will is important. And while more than half of people recognize the impor-tance of wills, our data shows that fewer people are thinking about estate planning than in 2019.

The chaos that ensues when there is no will or directives left behind is not something I would wish on anyone. Often, if the deceased person has been clear about their wishes, interpersonal conflict between survivors is averted. (Unless, of course, difficult people still choose to be difficult.)

Even if you don't feel you have enough to bequeath to be concerned about, find a form online and record your wishes. It is an act of love towards your survivors.

Speaking of love, you can also include emotions in this process by creating a statement of the contents of your heart. Such statements can include wishes for important people in your life, animals, letters for loved ones—the more comprehensive and detailed, the better.

People leave videotaped messages for loved ones for certain times in their lives. Parents have left a gift for each year, with a handwritten letter, for birthdays or other important dates. This can be a beautiful act of love.

Frequently, when we address these more practical sides of end of life with someone we are close to or are companioning, we find that it is as if a valve has been unstuck, allowing them to let their thoughts and feelings flow more easily than in those previously awkward or difficult conversations.

Bottom line, attending to the business of creating a will and other directives is the smart and responsible action for all of us to take. Taking care of business can help us tiptoe into the more emotionally provocative conversations surrounding end of life.

Trust that, by gently encouraging these conversations, you may be easing the tension around speaking about death.

It would be an error of omission if I did not mention that, more and more, we are finding there are end-of-life options for people who have a life-limiting condition and meet extensive criteria. This is an area it would be helpful to become proactively literate in. One place you can begin is hearing from someone who has closely walked that walk. On *The Death Dialogues Project* podcast Episodes 11 and 12, Jana Buhlmann shares her experience of walking beside her partner from his stage-four cancer diagnosis to his assisted death.

There are more and more accounts of end-of-life choice and assisted death available with a simple online search. As with this project, it can be very helpful to explore first-hand accounts rather than become overwhelmed by ethical and academic debates. Listen deeply to how your heart receives the information.

may we learn to sit with people's experiences, wishes and story, knowing that witnessing the deep crevices of another's existence requires a stillness of heart and mind

may we bravely show up and create plans for our own end of life and encourage those around us to do the same

may we engage in end-of-life planning, recognizing it is an intelligent choice and act of love for our loved ones

the long goodbye

holding to tomorrow
for if dreams die
tonight will be the last

asking not of what you give
for if dreams die
the gifts will wither through

loving with abandon
for if dreams die
our hope may follow swiftly

seeing you before me
for if dreams die
the last of you will too

may i sit at your side
and learn how it is
you want to die
before my dreams die
along with you

Much of the time, we are so centered on our own worlds and the business of life, we forget about the infinite scenarios that exist for death.

If you are reading this and your most recent loss was sudden, leaving echoes of trauma whispering in your ear, that may be your frame of reference for death, the lens through which you see death at the moment.

When we observe closely, we also see there is a subculture of actively dying folks who are on a journey toward their impending end of life. Many have been on this road for years while they live with a degenerative condition, terminal cancer or other terminal diagnosis.

It's not fair, but within this subculture are also infants and toddlers and children and teens. Out there in this parallel universe, people are living with the full knowledge that they are on the downward escalator that will deliver them to death's door sooner than they might have hoped. Sometimes the escalator may stall for a while, but other times they experience free-fall.

I recently had the only vivid dream I've ever experienced about being in such a situation, with a terminal diagnosis. The dream was heart- and eye-opening. I experienced a sensation of acute restriction, hearing from the medical folk that my prognosis was grim.

Last year, I had a nasty growth expanding inside me, making me feel very unwell. For about six months, a type of cancer was a possible diagnosis.

I was actually a little smug about my response. Instead of: *Why me?* I turned my response into: *Why not me?*

While I contemplated all of the unfairness that is felt and always will be felt after an untimely diagnosis, I made myself rest in the space of: *Why in the world would I think I would be exempt?*

Since the deaths of my soul-supports, I like to think I am so very down with death that I'll accept its invitation and look straight into its eyes as I'm waving goodbye to the ones left behind—barring a sudden death, where that opportunity would be taken from me.

This dream awakened something else in me.

I felt sudden, overwhelming dread.

Like, *really* felt it.

I felt a smidgen of the: *What will this actually feel like, what will be waiting, a whole new world or dark void? My loved ones on the other side? Or perpetual slumber?*

With this vivid dream, I was gifted with a nanosecond of actually *feeling* the pneumonia in my right lung, which was given as a secondary diagnosis, having my lifelong right-sided abdominal pain be announced as being less about the late diagnosis of Crohn's disease than the effects of a simmering tumor of a terminal cancer that was now on fire, growing daily, feasting on my life-force.

And there was an image of a light just outside my house at nighttime. An engine running, sending vibrations through the stark wooden home I stood in, car lights glowing through the cracks of the wooden slats, creating an ethereal illumination of the setting.

This car, this light, symbolized death, in the driver's seat, waiting for me.

My ride.

Just there.

Engine humming.

Was I really as comfortable with death as I profess? Could I actually walk out the door, smiling, give death a nod, and slither into the passenger seat?

And guess what? It wasn't a sense of overwhelming ease and *why not me* that I was feeling in those moments. Part of me, feeling panic, wanted to be reassured that I had a choice to take peaceful actions that would end my life if my existential and physical pain became too much.

I could sense the ease I might experience if I knew that choice about my death was a viable option. In essence, having the choice would allow me to know when it was the right time to open that car door and become death's passenger.

Or I might not choose that at all.

In fact, there might not be a time that running and jumping into death's waiting arms would feel appealing. That also felt strangely comforting. Having a sense of choice placated me.

Part of me was embarrassed by the realization that I might not be quite as down with death as I had proclaimed.

Suddenly I was processing all the things I'd hoped to still do with my wild and precious life and was assaulted by the realization that these choices, actions, and experiences were being taken from me.

The dream prompted me to send a grateful shout-out to the universe for opening up my personal understanding to what it might feel like to be informed of life's expiration date.

The real learning comes from understanding there is a world of people out there, living their own unique, long goodbye. We can expand by listening to the stories that many are able to share, while understanding that others will prefer to hold their story closely to them and disappear quietly into the dark night.

Maybe you've experienced a long goodbye.

Maybe you could learn more from those who are walking that walk now.

Speaking with people who have endured the long goodbyes has enriched my understanding of the world of those who live with extended caretaking—people like Hope Cross, whose young husband, Steve, had ALS and died after she cared for him for nine years. Understanding the trauma that can come with ongoing hyper-vigilance and medical emergencies has made me a better human. It makes me look at people who are walking this walk more compassionately. Many are mourning their person while they are still alive, witnessing a bit of them leaving every day. (You can hear a conversation with Hope recorded a month after her husband died on *The Death Dialogues Project Podcast,* Episode 74.)

There are so many ways the long goodbyes show up.

The person who is given an *incurable* prognosis, told she has a short time to live, but finds it enough time to process the end of life with her loved ones and say her goodbyes.

The parent who sees an infant's normal development suddenly begin to regress on a daily basis, only to learn the baby has a terminal degenerative disease.

The parents who must decide about harsh chemotherapy treatments while watching cancer's tentacles envelop their child.

Our stories are as unique as our fingerprints, and there is no specific one that defines anticipatory grief and the long goodbye. But by understanding the possibility it may enter our lives, we may be less confused if, and when, it visits.

As previously noted, one of my personal experiences with a long goodbye and anticipatory grief involved my mother, who lived with us the final two years of her life.

Unlike my brother, for whom we had held out hope for a miracle until the very end, my mother was 92 when she arrived to live with us. At best we knew that death was hovering— just there—and the magic and mystery of end of life was something unpacked on a regular basis.

After my brother's brain cancer diagnosis, never experiencing a moment of confusion, she began to narrate her own march to death.

Throughout our lives she had chirped out the mantra, "a mother should never outlive their child," even though she had repeatedly witnessed it happening with others.

We periodically recorded goodbyes for the rest of the family in the nine months following my brother's death. But much like that feeling I experienced in my dream, she would get right to the precipice of surrendering into death's arms and then pull back a small bit, contemplating that she might be willing to stay on the planet a little longer.

These months were filled with lamenting about her parenting of her children and keeping us in the house with a father she considered a monster. She had great difficulty reckoning with much of her life. Even her faith, her very identity, was questioned. She developed an understanding that what her children experienced at the hands of her husband was not "God's will."

As they say, hindsight is 20-20. She acknowledged that, before the advent of women's shelters, she was too afraid to move us permanently from our chaotic home life. I reassured her that much of that fear stemmed from her early life of poverty during the Great Depression.

Though lacking an ability to be emotionally present or a nurturer, my father was one thing: a hard worker. A provider. We had shelter. We had food, something she went without at times as a child.

The pavement laid down in our earlier days is easily forgotten, and sometimes it takes death knocking before we are able to see how those puzzle pieces of our past fit with the choices we've made.

Oh, this was painful ground.

Working towards my psychological and therapeutic training, I was forced, understandably, to unpack and analyze my childhood, and I never hesitated to revisit issues with a therapist if they resurfaced. Over the past couple of decades I had felt a sense of resolution and had largely let go of resentment about my childhood.

Enter my mother, repeatedly admonishing my father and his behaviors while conducting her end-of-life reviews. "I hope I don't have to see him after I die. If I see him coming I will run and hide. I will not be with him."

Even in her last few hours of life, when she was no longer alert or coherent but calling out an occasional "Mama," she exclaimed, "Tell them all I'm sorry."

I immediately knew who she was referring to— me and my brothers.

Tell them I'm sorry for keeping them in that house.

Tell them I'm sorry for not protecting them.

Tell them I'm sorry for thinking that I could not provide for you all without him.

Tell them I'm sorry for suggesting we could pray the abuse away.

Tell them I'm sorry for the days and nights of fear that formed their childhood.

Tell them I'm sorry. It's taken death to shine the light of truth on my living.

As illustrated here, the long goodbyes are fertile ground for the dying to land on unresolved issues and emotional pain and complicated stories. I share my mother's example to highlight the fact that, as people's lives are winding down, many are silently processing issues. Programmed to remain silent, they may never share openly. Having an awareness that internal end-of-life reviews are possibly ticking away may illuminate what we are observing with them, such as mood changes, a need to talk more or less, wanting to contact certain people, emotional withdrawal and so on.

As the exhaustion of death sets in, there's little energy left for intense processing. Let this be a reminder to ask the more complicated questions or engage in the complex conversations you know you'd like to have with your loved ones much earlier, if possible.

Is it possible that we may fail to inquire and support openly during these times because we are fearful of what may come up? Certainly.

This is unpredictable and emotionally layered terrain that may hold pain and trauma, *and* there will usually be stories of joy and satisfaction floating to the surface as well.

Long goodbyes are also an opportunity to witness the fragility of life and sit in the waterfall of love, remembrance and memory-making, and have those conversations surrounding end of life, so you, and they, may walk into the final stage of living cleansed and open.

As the complicated stories highlight, long goodbyes may be a time for soul-searching, getting responses to long-unanswered questions, and seeking resolution for the broken or missing parts of your stories.

If you feel there are deep injuries within your relationship with a person whom you must show up for at the end of their life, and you feel you would not be able to show up compassionately, consider inviting them to work through these issues while they are alive and healthier.

Based on the stories reported to me, as well as my own experience, the deathbed is best considered a reverent, sacred space for the dying—no matter their omissions in life—not a space for interpersonal conflict to hijack the experience.

It's fair to be human and have big and sometimes hurtful emotions; dying makes no one a saint, and there will always be complicated pasts.

It's also fair that if challenging emotional ground needs to be covered, it is in everyone's best interest to do so while your loved one is alive and in a condition to fully participate.

I've facilitated leaving letters with the deceased loved one's body that cover issues that had been painful, but I have not condoned reading a list of their errors to a dying person. It's my belief we all deserve dignified energy surrounding our exits, as we do during our time of arrival on this planet.

Depending on your relationships, it may be helpful to be aware of the dynamic of wanting a loved one to *finally show up* for you before their death. To understand that it can be a normal response to difficult relationships. Frequently, people hold out hope upon hope that before the person dies they might come around and be more of the gentle and caring person in their life they'd always hoped for.

The same goes for the dying person expressing hope. I've heard time and again the hope that love and care and respect would finally show up at their deathbed when there has been a history of upheaval within the family.

Surely, since I'm dying, my family will gather around me in love and leave the drama at the door.

One of the saddest things is to see people show up at the deathbed in conflict or exhibiting behavior that diminishes the ability of the loved one to experience serenity at the end of their life.

One experience I witnessed was an adult child, an addict, showing up and stealing the dying person's medication and money and then disappearing, without a goodbye. Another was an adult child insisting on pulling the dying elderly parent into family drama at the end of their life—an act that served no purpose but made their final days full of emotional turmoil and unrest.

If you have a complicated family, please consider having a family meeting and setting some ground rules and boundaries about how you all will show up for your dying person.

You commonly hear from people who work in this field that people usually die the way they lived. Having realistic expectations of the dying loved one may go a long way toward protecting your tender heart.

One beautiful practice for the person experiencing a long goodbye can be a gathering of loved ones while they are still alive. Some call it a living funeral. Others call it a party. Sometimes people correlate it with their birthday.

One woman with whom I conducted end-of-life Dignity Therapy told me she'd had a huge birthday party and stood on a table to read out her narrative document about her life created from that therapeutic intervention. Her face was beaming as she shared her joy in communicating so openly with the crowd assembled to *love her home.*

A goodbye gathering can certainly be healing, letting the person enjoy attention focused on their *living.* Who couldn't benefit from hearing beautiful words about the impact you've made on others' lives *before* you die? Clearly this type of activity has the potential to invite creativity and fun and camaraderie and focuses on what the dying person would love to be surrounded by.

Kate Manser, of the project *You Might Die Tomorrow*, would find it an error of omission if we failed to consider that death may come at any time. Therefore, we need to live our life mindfully, including those things that expand us, and conduct our relationships in a way that never takes our time together for granted. You can listen to her on Episode 30 and Episode 113 of our podcast to hear how death shattered her and then left her with a renewed, refreshing perspective on life.

may we find the courage and love to serve as companion when those we love are experiencing the long goodbye

may we hold ourselves gently, processing our own feelings that may arise, and appreciate our loved ones deeply when we find ourselves in the long goodbye.

may we find a willingness to embrace our own long goodbye, should our death arrive in that manner, acknowledging this sacred time of life

should they stay or
should they go now

within the house you lived
you stayed after your death
minutes, hours, days
loving, weeping, mirth
music was our guide
tender memories
color returning to your face
a smile, they said
your finger curving just so
the birthmark we share
we were given enough of you
to feel our goodbye
gently in our bones
this was how history
had long served death
a community of love
holding your body with grace
stories of all that you were
having time to percolate
poured into the communal cups
we passed and shared
no one could have prepared us
for what these days held
a precious memory
that now lives
forever in our hearts
just alongside
your love

One day, the death of someone you adore will happen. Maybe it already has, and that is why you are here.

Death may come charging in: loud, dramatic, and shocking.

It may whisper gently into the ear of your loved one as they sleep.

It may exist on the other side of the telephone, when we receive a shocking call.

It may be you that will bear witness to a previously incomprehensible scene of death.

In all likelihood, however death announces itself, it will bring you to your knees.

In this section we will discuss primarily a possibility that could occur when an expected death has happened within the home, of a person who has asked for no heroic life-extending measures and DNR (do not resuscitate).

Shortly before my brother's death, I watched a documentary based on Zenith Virago's long career as a DeathWalker called *Zen and the Art of Dying*. She, very practically, introduced me to the first step involved if someone you know is dying does so within your setting.

Refrain from calling the emergency number.

Instead, *put the kettle on*. There is no emergency. When a person dies whose death is anticipated, *expected*, with instructions of no resuscitation— their death is not an emergency. There is no need to quickly dial for an ambulance.

This can be a difficult concept for many folks to accept. Our immediate impulse may be to reach for the phone; that is our learned response.

The time between their death and when their body departs your home can be very special indeed. Just as your loved one experienced their last exhale, your time is marked to have a deep state of release and stillness, and your own exhale before *the professionals* take over, if that is your plan.

Sit quietly with your loved one.

Speak aloud to them if you like.

Hold their hand.

Gather others and have your own personal time of goodbye within your space.

Maybe you want to bathe them with oils or their favorite essence, comb their hair the way they liked it, and dress them as they desired, or in a way that resonates.

Maybe you just need an hour with them.

Maybe you find you want them home longer, like we and so many people I've spoken with did, cherishing that time of staying close.

I rushed to the United States from New Zealand when my brother took a sudden turn and was dying. I mentioned to his wife that, if he happened to die before I arrived, it wasn't an emergency. I encouraged her to have some time with him before any services were called, expressing that it could be very meaningful.

New Zealand, where we've lived since 2011, has a strong cultural foundation in honoring death in a very personal way, thanks to the Maori culture. Keeping the body close, where people stay with their deceased loved one and process their loss at their Iwi's (tribe or group descended from a common ancestor) Marae (cultural/spiritual gathering place). Having the body home is also a common practice. Three days is the typical amount of time to be with the body of the deceased, but I've heard stories of longer.

Because of the cultural example of the Maori, many Pakeha (non-Maori New Zealander) have adapted the practice of keeping their loved ones close as well. Therefore, no one in New Zealand bats an eye about doing death differently (except, possibly, the traditional funeral home businesses).

This understanding of doing death differently is what empowered me to mention the possibility to my brother's wife in the United States. We knew that caring for him and keeping him at home was not common practice, but what did we have to lose to inquire?

Much like what may be done searching for a home-birth-friendly practitioner, after my arrival I asked the hospice social worker what funeral home she thought would be the most flexible regarding keeping his body home.

When my brother died, and after we cared for his body and dressed him, I called the suggested funeral director.

His response: "We haven't been involved with people choosing not to embalm or keep their loved ones home, but I realize this is a coming trend and I will support you in any way possible. You can keep him home as long as you'd like. Call us day or night when you are ready for him to be picked up and we will be there within an hour."

That response, friends, was viscerally comforting, and one I hope all funeral industry workers become comfortable with—setting aside any thoughts of threat to their income. Meeting people that seek answers, from a place of gentle inquiry, problem-solving, and deep compassion.

He then informed me where the main places were on my brother's body to keep him cool with freezer blocks (under his head and over his abdomen). My sweet brother stayed home with us for three days. We called to have him picked up the evening before the funeral, which would be held in their small country church. The funeral home transporters came around 11 p.m., in response to our call as promised.

This was my first experience with having a loved one's body stay within the home, and our family had a transformative time of processing, connection, reminiscing, laughing, crying, music, singing, writing notes for him—honestly, it was love in action.

Some people didn't want to leave his side much at all.

Some people only glanced in and then spent time with the people working on food and story boards and telling tales.

My brother's youngest two children were 16 and 20, and they have quite reflective, low-key personalities. It was anybody's guess how they might react to this arrangement, and honestly, it was them and his wife that were my primary concern from the moment he took leave of his body.

Their mom would circle around occasionally, asking, "Are you ready for Dad to leave yet?" I was always a bit surprised when they would quickly shake their heads no.

Part of me wondered, mournfully: *How are we ever going to be able to part with his body?*

And then something happened on that final evening that I've heard others speak of within this timeframe.

My sister-in-law sidled up to me and whispered, "I think it's time."

Yes, the kids could handle that.

We gathered by candlelight around him, and the guitar was played and our voices rang out as the mood became more solemn, contemplating this farewell to his body. I imagined wailing and people emotionally disintegrating as he left.

Surprisingly, that did not happen.

As he was rolled out of the house on a stretcher, he passed by all of the family members that were in the home at that time. People reached out. Touched him. I didn't hear crying.

His wife, our oldest brother and I followed him outside and watched as he was driven away. My heart was being pulled out of my body as his physical presence left us, as I sensed was the case for them as well, but then we walked into the house into … wait, what was that we were hearing?

Laughter. People filling their plates with food. There was almost

72

the feeling you might see at the meal after a communal barn-raising. An overriding sense of a job well done.

And I know, deep in our hearts, our experience unfolded into something my brother would have absolutely treasured, harking back to the ways of our forbears. A man who lived much of his life connected to the ways of the olden days; we knew we had made him proud.

I interviewed New Zealander Rebecca Tingey, who shared the story of the sudden death of her partner in a paragliding accident. She described how his body was brought home and tucked into a bed at his parents' home. She slept next to him every night. Josh was embalmed, and Bex was blown away by the amazing job the funeral home had done, thrilled she could have extended time with him.

"He looked as though he was sleeping and would soon wake up," she said.

Friends and family gathered throughout these days, up until the funeral. People would come and go. His mates might have a beer as they shared stories. Then, because Josh's funeral was over a holiday weekend, he was brought back home after the funeral.

The funeral home staff asked where she would like her partner. "Back in bed, please." They did just that, which gave her two more nights to spend with him, and she treasured that time. The time before the funeral was full of people coming and going. This was her time with her love. "The time I had alone with him before he was cremated was invaluable."

You can hear her story in detail on our podcast, Episode 72, "Our Lost Adventure," and the following bonus episode: "After Death: keeping our loved ones home."

If you've previously engaged in traditional funeral home services, it can resonate deeply when you hear alternative ways of dealing with the aftermath of the death of a dear loved one. Historically, in funeral home settings, your loved one is kept alone and family is given a limited amount of time to spend with them, sometimes being charged for the visitation sessions. You are in a public place, being watched by staff. There just isn't the opportunity to really unwind and let your feelings naturally come up.

Visitations can be a blur as you are having to stand while people pass through the line of family, giving their condolences. And the funeral is much the same. Families frequently express that they felt on display.

Time spent in a personal space or home with your loved one after a death can cover so much important ground for the grief process.

Within our experience, I remember the kids standing over their dad at home and me, whispering to their mother, "This right here? These three days are worth three years of therapy."

Do the stars have to align to make such a choice? Quite possibly.

Now we have a whole wave of end-of-life workers building who can assist you in making those stars align. You can listen to the podcasts listed at the end of this book and become more familiar with the work, which can vary from provider to provider. These are relationships to forge proactively, rather than reactively, if you are given the gift of time. Having the advocacy and guidance that accompany this type of service can be extremely comforting and beneficial to the entire process, no matter what your vision is of the outcome you desire.

Clearly, you need cooperation from all involved. And there are deaths that involve so much trauma that having the body open to everyone may not be realistic. But in those cases, in cultures that practice the home time, the body could simply be in a closed casket, which may be your family's preference anyway.

There are instances where people have had their loved one's bodies brought home from the hospital or hospice or other medical facility after their death, or from a funeral home. Even with coroner involvement, people have been able to make the home vigil time work for them. This is certainly an area where proactive planning may make the entire process flow smoothly.

How we handle our loved ones' bodies after death is another practice modern culture has taken from us. After the embalming of

President Abraham Lincoln, so that his body could ride on a viewing train from Washington D.C. to Springfield, Illinois, with stops along the way for the public to pay their respects, the business of funerals and embalming escalated. As happens when business intervenes with nature, some motives will be more economically driven than aligned with the greater good of all.

Explore.

Have the conversations about your loved one's wishes. Listen to or read stories of alternative ways to handle death.

And ultimately?

Follow your big, beautiful, aching heart.

As you might imagine, taking that initial pause with my brother after his death led to the most deeply meaningful time many members of my family had ever experienced surrounding end of life.

Through walking that walk, I was strengthened to do the same for my mother, as she requested, nine short months later.

As you hear examples of how people have done death differently, keep in mind that these are simply ideas. Stories. In no way are they meant to be directives about one way being better than another way.

When it comes to birth and death, each individual has to pick what works best for them. My last child was born at home, which I had previously desired. Does that mean I have a standard of *all things natural* for birth that I believe everyone should strive for? Absolutely not.

Birth and death are monumental transitions in our lives. First and foremost, you need to listen to your own heart, following the path that seems right for you.

You may choose a scheduled caesarean birth. You may choose to have the body of your deceased person immediately removed from your home and taken under the care of a mortician and funeral home.

Those are very personal choices.

What I have heard over and over again regarding death practices out of the mainstream is that people do not realize we have choice about how we handle end of life and post-death care.

Not every more natural choice surrounding death will be an option, due to rules, regulations and guidelines that may exist in your locale. But if hearing those stories brings up a niggle in your heart to explore options, let that be your motivation to check into possibilities.

If you are curious to hear more about keeping loved ones home after death, please listen to the relevant podcast episodes listed at the end of the book.

may we consider sharing end-of-life thoughts and feelings with our loved one, and ask to hear theirs, for it brings potential for a deeper connection of understanding and love

may we bravely inquire and advocate for our choices if we find ourselves wanting to do death and the aftermath differently

may we be open to the different ways people choose to do death

the crash: they. are. gone

it is because we have felt

immeasurable love

we feel overwhelming grief

help us find the blessing

within the paradox

help us understand why

the world still turns without them

I can't count how many times people have expressed the shock over how, when they next saw the light of day after their person died, they couldn't believe the world was still moving along as it always had, as if nothing happened.

Busses are stopping at their stops. Children are on their way to school. People carrying their groceries.

The disbelief.

The outright horror.

Our knowledge that life will never be the same.

The audacity that people can continue to walk in the world as if nothing happened.

Don't you know that my world has forever changed?

The space we inhabit just after witnessing or learning of someone's death is a surreal landscape. Rather than denial—the first stage Elizabeth Kubler-Ross identified for people who have been diagnosed with a terminal illness—I think it looks more like disbelief and a gut-wrenching longing for it not to be true.

Yes, an audacious disbelief that the rest of the world continues to tick on.

Of course, when you receive a terminal diagnosis it would be understandable to have lots of energy being put into: *No, it can't be that bad, I'll be the outlier statistic; something went wrong with the testing; no! I refuse to accept this is happening.*

Denial.

When you witness the last breath of your beloved or see their dead body, there's really no denying your loved one has died.

Initially, children may have some magical thinking, but even they will wake up to the permanence of the absence of their person. But the *longing.* The absolute *gut-aching wish* that this was not true is quite universal.

Those initial hours do frequently have a common thread of disbelief.

How can someone be here one moment and gone the next?

Therein exists a variety of anguish that brings you to your knees. A visceral, physical emotion, a feeling that your heart is being wrung out. You look outside and see the world continuing to move. Maybe you get a mundane phone call from a telemarketer, or someone calls just to chat and you want to scream—*Wait a minute, doesn't the world know my person died?*

Nothing else matters.

There are so many common threads between the birth and death transitions, beautiful and horrible.

My thoughts when I had my first baby were not just: *Aw, isn't she beautiful?* It was a euphoria, because we had both survived after being close to the veil. This may be similar to how one would feel reaching the summit of Everest intact.

And I recall that, while being wheeled out to go home, I had that feeling of awe and respect for every woman I saw, every woman in my life, every woman who had ever given birth: *How can all of these women do that?* Nothing could have prepared me for the intensity and challenge of it all.

After experiencing intimate, deep loss for the first time, the feeling was similar. Suddenly a world opens up that had never *really* been understood.

You may think about all the people who've experienced gut-wrenching, tragic loss and wonder how they continue to put one foot in front of the other. And, although it's cold comfort at the time, as you think of them, you realize you are part of a new club and your life will never be the same.

The naive coasting through life is gone. You fully recognize that your people, *you,* may die at any moment. You may find yourself dreading the next loss while still in the throes of your current loved one's demise.

In the throes of acute loss, sleeping with my mother on a pallet on the floor of my brother's basement on the night of my father's death, I said to her: *Please, don't die before me, I want to go next,* anticipating how excruciating it would feel to see her die after experiencing such intensity over my less-attached parent's death.

never quite prepared

Even if your loved one has been unwell for a long time and officially received a poor prognosis, you may be surprised by your shock after they die. The impact of the death may even embarrass you. *Shouldn't I have been prepared? He's been unwell for so long.*

You may have been actively planning your person's end of life and the aftermath, with or without them, but our humanness can shove all practicalities to the corner, and you may find yourself shaking your head in disbelief. *I had no idea it would feel like this.*

Circumstances surrounding a death can affect our initial reaction.

When our person is killed suddenly—an untimely death—our minds can initially take over to protect us.

One woman interviewed for *The Death Dialogues Project*, Beth Robbins, waited and waited for her husband to return home. The later it became, the more she wondered: *Has something happened?* Then the police car pulled into her driveway and two policemen came to the door, and she refused to answer the knock.

If I didn't answer it, he wouldn't be dead.

Here is an excerpt from Beth Robbins' book, *A Grief Sublime*, reprinted with permission:

Police lights. In my driveway. Flashing. Red lights.

I am in my pajamas. It is ten at night. The glass of white wine on the coffee table is untouched. Steve is hours late. The lights flash red.

I think: don't answer the door.

I hear a car door slam. Then another.

Two men are on my porch. They are under the light from the porch. They are outside my screen door. Under the golden light from the porch. The red lights flash from their car. And they see me.

I turn to stone. This is not my story.

This cannot be my story.

This is my story:

It was just this morning. Steve ran out. Smiling. Noah and I were late to school. I waved. Impatient. No time to pause for a hug, or another wave. I'll see you tonight after my meeting he called out.

This is my story: I stood in front of my students. I quoted Dante.

I quoted Annie Dillard.

I spoke about attentiveness. I spoke about the world sparking and flaming. I spoke about being lost but with attention finding a way out. Out of the truth we live in a created world.

This is my story. Or, rather, this was my story. But then it wasn't my story.

Steve didn't arrive home.

And a police car in the driveway. And then a knock on the door. If I don't open the door this will not be my story.

My story will pick up as it had been.

Like this:

He will come home. I will drink the wine. He will eat coffee ice cream.

But they knock again. The officers stand outside my screen door.

Under the light from the porch. They see me.

There is a feeling of unreality. A haunting. I feel I've stepped outside of life and am entering another realm.

I ignore the men outside.

But they do not leave.

I watch myself outside of myself.

I see myself pull my robe closed. The movements agonizingly slow. I see myself move from the couch toward the men.

I open the door ...

By sharing her reaction, Beth illustrates that flash in time when death can have the most rational of us suddenly overtaken with a sort of hopeful disbelief. This type of reaction has been repeated over and over in stories collected for the project. It isn't about losing touch with reality; it's about trying to hit pause on the fact that your heart knows that your reality is forever changed.

Your mind can play tricks on you. Be open to recognizing when it happens, and be kind to yourself about it.

Parents who have had children die speak of a lengthy state of not fully comprehending their child's absence in their day-to-day physical life. The shock of losing an adult or even an elder can feel overwhelming, but the loss of our child, no matter their age, is picking a fight with the order of things. Whether it is in utero, stillbirth, a protracted condition or a sudden, unexpected death, every parent spoken with for this project has experienced a devastating emotional response; a disassembling of their very selves. We will later discuss how a traumatic loss can add complicated chapters to our adjustment process.

At 95, my mother's death was impending and there was no denying it; we just didn't know exactly when, until she decided it was time.

After Mom's death, which largely mimicked my brother's dying process, but faster, we cared for her as we had my brother.

There had been so much mindful lead-up, so much intimate care of her end of life, and yet, as close as I was to her for those four days after her death, while she remained home with us, there were still times I would wake up from a doze and expect her to sit up and speak to me.

But it was preparing to shroud her for her journey to the crematorium when the reality of it all brought me to my knees.

We love lavender and grow it at our home. I had the thought to harvest long lavender fronds and have them wrapped with her body so the aroma would intermingle with her physical essence as it wafted away on the breeze. Something about that physical action of harvesting those fronds brought the permanence of her death home in a deeper way.

In those moments, I felt connected to my ancestors, and all the carers and nurturers who had taken care of life's transitions throughout centuries. The poignancy of my active participation in releasing the woman who'd birthed me created an intense awareness of the circle of life and death that overcame me.

The wails came from a place deep inside that I had never met before.

I didn't want my mama to leave.

She'd tried to prepare me for this moment—*promise me you won't miss me and grieve for too long*—but I'm here to tell you, friend, nothing can prepare you for communing intimately with death on the day your love is no longer walking on the planet. Equally so, you may find a numbness or lack of initial emotional response daunting. And there will be a few of you who float on relief and joy for your loved one. Yes, we are all so very different.

Whether it's your dear child who has gone before you, your loved one with a protracted illness, a dreaded phone call of shock and horror, or an aged person who doesn't wake up one morning, please remember, you are not alone in that state of shock and disbelief.

may we understand that this time of shock is a time of unlearning everything about life we thought was predictable

may we embrace the concept of "enoughness" and understand that, right now, it is enough to show up to life and take what lies immediately before us one minute, one hour, one day at a time

may we ask for what we need

meet your new life partner:
grief

in the middle of the night
after your first great loss
you walk through the world differently
innocence fleeting is now obscured
laugh lines remain
reminding you of what life
was like before you realized that
everything you've ever loved
could be gone in one split second
stars now speak to you
dreams hold visits held in layers
some revealed
some held tight
mystery holds your hand
random answers to unasked questions
and in all the torturous pain
there is one constant
the only comfort to tuck you in at night
great loss could not knock on our door
had there not been fathomless connection
stories that volumes could never hold
and the deepest of love

You may already know each other intimately, but let me introduce you to your new life partner: *grief.*

Adjustment.

An exhale.

Bereavement.

Heartbreak.

Anguish.

Sorrow.

Desolation.

Denial.

Compartmentalization.

Cracked wide open.

Numbness.

Detachment.

Relief.

There are many words you might use, at varying times, to describe your emotional terrain related to the death of your loved one.

The word *grief* can also represent a transformational time when many come to terms with magical aspects of life on the planet, and beyond, that change the way they walk in the world.

Years ago, in my psychology training, we were basically taught two words: *grief* and *bereavement.* And within those, the minimal lessons were less about understanding and more about how to pathologize.

There was no discussion about how one's grief process will be as unique to them as their fingerprint.

I do not recall the conversations reminding us that every human will experience deep loss and grief in our lives. Or the possibility that another's grief might trigger our own.

No, grief was discussed as something that happens to someone else.

We missed the bit about the universality of grief and that death levels the playing field, no matter your credentials or socioeconomic status. We will all be brought to our knees by the aftermath of death at some point in our lives—through deep processing and also glimmers of the magical connection that remains for some of us.

The topic of grief and loss were barely covered, cultivating denial within the same professional realm that has spawned the medical world's whacked-out relationship with death. *If we don't talk about it, maybe it won't happen; maybe we can magically avoid death.*

Deep denial of the end of life did not serve us well in our training. Within the clinical setting, the goal is to save lives, which means bypassing invaluable lessons about the end of life. Yet that's where we need to grow literacy.

Naturally, experience tells us that death also happens in clinical settings, but even now I hear from trainee clinicians, in medicine and the helping fields, that there isn't enough focus on it. Therefore, we are often inadequately skilled or uncomfortable about meeting the needs of dying patients and their families in a meaningful way.

My earlier nursing school experience covered grief and loss more than my psychological training did; it was also a bit more real about being at the bedside of the dying. That was because I had an excellent instructor—which is always about the luck of the draw.

Since, as a society, we don't bring death out of the closet, we also don't speak much about grief—what it looks and feels like, the surprising ways it might show up, how individual it is to each relationship.

How it is not just one-size-fits-all contained in that word: *grief.*

I'm sorry if you were not prepared for the intensity of your emotions in the aftermath of death. Few of us are. Especially since we live in a world that thinks it is morbid or taboo to speculate about what it might feel like for specific people in our lives to die, or to speak with our loved ones about how they might feel when death comes.

Let's acknowledge the basic premise: everyone grieves.

Next: everyone grieves *differently.*

Early grief can look different from extended grief, as we've discussed when speaking about the utter shock that can initially accompany a death. And yes, depending on the relationship we had with the person, and who the person was in our life, our grief reaction will be different.

What was the death like?

Was it traumatic to experience it with your person?

Was it expected?

Was it a shock to your system?

Was it your baby, your child, your soulmate, a sibling or an elderly parent?

These experiences will all be different, but the common thread among them is the love that made the deceased special to you and will continue to beat in your own heart.

Next, we will look at some areas of grief. You will not find these in the DSM, the bible for diagnosing mental health conditions. These are born in the stories of the people that have been shared throughout the years, as if a web of a spider called *love* has connected the emotions and experience of the aftermath of death into its own individual design.

Unpredictable.

No two are alike, like a snowflake.

May you be open to honoring your process of grieving, showing up to yourself as you would a beloved friend.

help me now

For those of you who might be frantically searching the pages of this book for the answers to grief—*the cure*—I am sorry to report that there is none.

Many people attempt to escape their anguish, succumbing to the culture's hypnotic plea of *get over it,* practicing the same compartmentalization they have probably applied to difficult emotions throughout their lives. Filing away *the hard.*

People like me, and probably you, just can't do that. Deep feelers must let grief have its way with us.

As for the stuffers, the *get-on-with-it* folks—grief will have its way with them as well, but it may come out lopsided. There are folks who will experience a less intense reaction because of a belief system they've developed or engaged in. Then, it may look like more of an *adjustment period* than the sore emotions we think of as accompanying grief.

Get-on-with-it folks might hide their reactions in compulsive behaviors—too muchness. Too much work or alcohol or substances or rage, or isolation that morphs into depression, or whatever it is for the individual that can bang a drum louder than the echoes of their loss.

But it's a common belief that we, the *wallowers*, the ones to whom people will long to implore, "Can't you move on already?" are actually the ones who are letting grief have its way with us.

Just today I heard from a parent who had found their young-adult child who died by overdose a couple of months earlier. They were feeling tortured, wondering if they would ever feel alive again.

Haunted by the image of finding their child. Aching for what will never be. Tearing themselves apart for not finding a way to save that child.

This process will totally dismantle them. You can understand why someone in that position might feel like giving up at times. It can feel so hard and unsurmountable.

Please try to remember that the taking-apart of you that is happening in the throes of deep loss is a *normal* part of the process. It will be slow and it will be painful, *and* eventually there will be a time when you actually have a choice of how you want to be put back together.

When you can start imagining what that transformation might look like, that's your little bell tinkling, like in the movie *It's a Wonderful Life*, that signaled an angel getting their wings. For you, that little bell signals: *My love's death and the love we have together is growing something new inside me.*

Maybe you start noticing that the beautiful memories are taking up more space in your brain than the tragic ones.

Maybe it's as simple as how you walk in the world.

Maybe you find yourself becoming filled with more compassion for others who have had similar experiences.

Or maybe it's who you will now reach out to or give your time.

It may be what art you decide to finally make or do, in a different way.

As you will see in these pages, it sometimes heralds massive personal transformation. That's been witnessed by many of the folks interviewed for this project.

That process takes time.

Early on is the incubation period, where you need to cocoon yourself gently, taking great care of your basic needs. Death, and what grief asks of you, can be utterly exhausting.

Your body needs rest, nourishment, hydration, gentle holding.

Your mind needs a break. Work on releasing the *what ifs,* the regret, beating yourself up, obsessive thinking about the process of the person's dying.

Your heart needs *love*.

One small practice that has provided great relief in those early days is simple: Take a moment alone, put some relaxing music on if you can (not mandatory), and feel yourself grounded into your body. Then begin taking nice, even breaths, in and out. Try to establish a rhythm of five to six counts in and five to six counts out. The number of seconds isn't as important as keeping the breath even. Make it a comfortable, doable rhythm.

With each exhalation, mindfully imagine your love leaving your heart and landing in the heart of your deceased loved one. And on the inhale, imagine their love coming into your heart. Try to stay with this practice for five to ten minutes.

Consider using this when you find your mind is taking over. Use it before you get out of bed, upon awakening, and prior to going to sleep. Use it when you need a break from it all. Use it when your heart is longing to the point of aching.

Pause, and use it now.

There are great benefits to your physical heart from this practice, and it can be seen as a possible antidote to a very real phenomenon: broken-heart syndrome, or Takotsubo cardiomyopathy. This breathing and visualization process works at increasing your heart rate variability (HRV) and regulating your autonomic nervous system (ANS), which is a healthy exercise for your heart and mind.

I was involved in a study of 150 participants using this type of technique in a cardiology practice.

There was the young, fit woman whose father died suddenly, and she ended up in the emergency room later that day with a myocardial infarction (MI), eventually diagnosed with broken-heart syndrome. There were people with fresh, deep grief. This technique was life-changing for many, from one session to the next.

As I might say to a client—*what do you have to lose?* It's a gentle, enjoyable process. And, hey, we have to breathe anyway.

May you make space for love and mindful breathing as you move through the layered processes that meet you after the death of your person.

traumatic grief

Trauma is defined differently for everyone.

What might be traumatic for you to witness and be involved with may not be so for the next person.

There are commonalities within the stories people have told, because that is where the truth lies.

With sudden deaths, you may witness the death or immediate aftermath. If you are not a witness, your imagination may take off, piecing together the parts of the story you have heard with the unknowns created in your mind.

No matter the age of the person, sudden deaths have one thing in common: They are untimely. Unexpected. Traumatic.

Sudden deaths from illness can bring trauma for those involved. Seeing your person in extended pain and suffering may be traumatic for you. Unexpectedly finding your loved one dead from an overdose or having ended their life is highly traumatic. Finding anyone dead, even from natural circumstances, can be traumatic.

Auto and other accidental deaths, murder, literally dropping dead that can happen at any age with unknown underlying conditions; the list is endless.

And what may seem an uncomplicated death to one person may cause a traumatic response in the next. We never want to hear from a professional or support person: *Oh, that shouldn't have bothered you so much.*

Being *should-ed* on or *should-ing* on ourselves is not a healthy practice and begs to be avoided.

For children of any age, seeing their parent, their loved one, vulnerable and deteriorating can be traumatic.

Of course we are traumatized. Suggesting it should be otherwise would be implying we are without a heart, like the Tin Man before he was blessed by Oz.

As much as we like to believe the messages about natural death being peaceful, it isn't always. Those last moments or days of your loved one's life can prove traumatizing to the observer.

Commonly, in experiences surrounding perceived trauma, we find ourselves having feelings and thoughts that are frequently associated with post-traumatic stress disorder (PTSD): revisiting the happenings in your mind; dreams/nightmares; difficult emotional responses being triggered by something in the environment or a memory; emotional detachment; excessive worry or obsessing; anxiety symptoms that can include anxiety/panic attacks. People have unique responses to traumatic stress.

Even though it was my highest honor to use my nursing background and undying love for my brother to provide bedside and end-of-life care, the experience shattered me.

Don't get me wrong. I loved the service I was providing for him and his family. Each and every moment in which love and connection flowed between us I remember as a tender, irreplaceable time. Honestly, I had never felt so strong and capable in my life. My own health issue, which can be triggered by stress, somehow remained stable through the year of his unpredictable decline.

It was the aftermath of his death that was relentless.

Returning to New Zealand after his death and walking into my mother's declarations that she should have gone first—and her processing of life-long regrets, many having to do with keeping us in the same house as our troubled father, while expressing her desire to exit the planet—provided a "perfect storm" of emotions that surely had its way with my grieving process. This was territory with my mother that my brother and I had always imagined we would be meeting together. And he was gone. My rock wasn't there to bounce ideas off of, or to help me process our mother's deterioration.

An infinite number of complicating factors make up our multifaceted lives and histories, which makes searching for an exact clinical label for our grief response next to impossible.

Speaking as a previous clinician myself, who was paid to tick the correct diagnostic boxes, it is unlikely we can ever deeply understand the full spectrum of one's emotional responses and how they affect the way a person is able to show up in the world.

There is no *typical* in the situation I've described, regarding my experience with my brother and immediate immersion into my mother's goodbye process and ensuing death, as there will be no *typical* in your story. What's most important is that we abandon trying to squeeze ourselves into a *typical* box when it comes to our emotional responses to a death in our lives.

As helpers, we need to spend more energy connecting deeply to the stories of the people we work with than playing the game of diagnostic roulette, which often disengages the clinician from the process of listening empathically.

After my return home, having been strong throughout the illness and dying process, I found myself experiencing flashbacks about my brother's incapacitation and his final week.

My brother had been my shelter and my rock throughout my entire life. Seeing your hero, a strong, healthy person, lose bits of themselves can take its toll. And it had for me. Then, walking right back into nine months of caring for my mother before and after her death, my grief was messy. In fact, my grief is quite indescribable because of the complex layers within our histories together and our relationships.

I'm reminded of the dynamic that I've witnessed and heard of repeatedly, when a parent has a very ill child who recovers. They remain stoic, strong, healthy, surviving easily on minimal sleep. Then, after the child recovers, they shatter.

We must assume that many of us are genetically wired for this: to have that inherent resolve that gets us through traumatic experiences. Then, when the space arrives for the exhale—be it after a recovery or a death— all bets are off on what the emotional and physical response will look like.

One approach I can recommend, if you find yourself in the throes of a response to trauma or complex grief that doesn't show signs of improvement, is a therapy called EMDR: Eye Movement Desensitization Reprocessing. It's a bit of magic and doesn't have you digging scarily deep into your entire life all at once. Rather, it works on individual troubling memories.

I went through training for EMDR after my people died. The first time our instructor asked for a volunteer, my hand flew up.

In front of an entire room of other therapists, I worked on the memory of my brother, incapacitated in a hospital bed, and experienced some immediate relief that has remained with me.

Yes, I still have surges of memories and grief, but I repeatedly hear from people that EMDR saved them. Notably, the World Health Organization (WHO) states that EMDR is the frontline therapy for trauma. Eye Movement Desensitization Reprocessing belies what we typically think of as therapy, focusing less on speaking and more on bringing up traumatic memories while the therapist provides a unique visualization experience. EMDR therapy helps the brain process these memories, and allows normal healing to resume

Further speaking to the differences in us all, while writing this, another brother, twenty-two months older than my previously deceased brother, was found dead.

In the circumstances of his death were all sorts of things I was sure would have brought me great trauma. He'd been dead for some time before he was found; he'd been alone; the exact circumstances of his death were unclear; and the postmortem examination information was not definitive. These were all factors, along with a complicated backstory, that I would have wagered would cause a traumatic grief response in me.

In fact, an almost immediate internal response, after hearing the news, was: *Please, please, don't let me dive into the depths of grief,* as I had after my other brother and mother's deaths. After finally beginning to feel I was coming up for air, I adamantly desired to keep my head above the deep, turbulent waters. Waters where grief can pull us under.

Much to my surprise, I have not slipped into a horrifically deep abyss, and I am grateful. My overwhelming sense has been one of *release*. Release for him, as I imagine him flying free and finally being at peace.

And yes, there has been a welcome sigh of relief that I have not been tortured by his death and the circumstances of it. I'd be remiss not to share that part of that equation was an almost immediate sign that I received after asking him to please let me know that he'd made it safely to the other side. Seconds later, that sign was received, when the New Zealand fantail bird appeared inside our home; the first time ever. According to Maori lore, a fantail in your home is the symbol of a deceased loved one coming to say good-bye.

This perspective, after my most recent intimate death experience, has been very welcome. I can only attribute it to the work done within an anticipatory grief process over the past five years, and through the work of this project, which opened me to the full spectrum of thoughts and feelings surrounding death. Giving me permission to *go there*, rather than hiding out in a cave of denial.

Much of my grieving him had been in process for a long time. Rather than ruminating over difficult times we'd experienced, love came riding in on its white horse, and I was overwhelmed with memories of his positive qualities and the wild fun we'd had together. He was a hilarious, self-proclaimed black sheep, with his inner child in the driver's seat, and life was certainly a roller-coaster ride with him. My reaction has been a testimony as to how the aftermath of death may even surprise us in a positive way.

When Claudia Crase first contacted me about her adult son who had ended his life, we wrote long emails to each other, her eloquence intermingled with her heartbreak. Her insight into his actions mesmerized me, having spent much of my career working with people who were contemplating or had attempted to end their lives, as well as having personal experience of this.

We became connected and have stayed in touch since her interview, as has happened with others who have shared their stories. This kind of emotional intimacy surrounding death creates a bond.

Not long ago, she sent the following writing to me. I immediately asked her if I could include it here so you could have a glimpse into her process, over a year after her son's death.

Her dear son, Tanner, ended his life in January 2019. Almost a year to the day after, she spoke with me for the podcast (Episode 47, "Reframing Suicide: a mother's story"), an episode I highly recommend for its staggering view of a mother's experience with her son, who had always struggled with being of this world while simultaneously showing outward success and pleasure in many things.

This writing is but a glimpse into her traumatic grief. I thank Claudia for giving us an opportunity to gaze inside her process, twenty months after his death:

The whir of a flitting hummingbird … an open vein … the swirling nebula of you. Every day a bit of something gets snagged on the essence of you. Today, I am browsing book titles, reading book jacket verbiage in the Country Bookshelf in downtown Bozeman, and there you are. Palpable. Ephemeral, yet intensely here. I'm looking for something to plunge into to assuage my panic as the pandemic continues and the insanity of "45" worsens daily. One plot line piques my interest: the protagonist lives a double life; one as an ordinary someone, another in a parallel Universe of superpowers, shadows, mystery, and meaning.

I'd love that to be true of you. A double reality: you've died, but you're fully alive, living out your magical you-ness in an alternate reality I can access. All I need to do is open the book and settle in for a damned good read. A title tugs at me; even the combination of a couple of words reveals your shape to me, inviting me to dance with you for a moment. This doesn't surprise me because you were a word person. You read. You and I talked ideas, books, the use and misuse of words. Fifteen minutes in a bookstore these days sets my heart and mind aswirl with you. I walk out without a book because the best story I can imagine is the story of you. All others disappoint.

Lately, when I've gotten snagged by a memory or dragged to the edge of the abyss of the loss of you, I have been able to think more analytically about your death. I have been able to think more critically about what you might have been experiencing. I have been able to reflect—rather than react. Ahh ... it's truer to say that I can sometimes choose if I'm going to give in to the reacting. If I'm going to immerse myself in the emotions of losing you. I do have more moments when I am able to roll the rawest parts of your death around in my mind. Why would I do this? Because I need to.

In these moments of reflecting, I am able to revisit that day on which the rest of my life hinges:

My memory sweeps over items you left out in your room: Single pages of writing you left beside your computer, your organized files, your last hand-written words. Those single pages—now phantoms—still tug at me. You left them out in plain sight. You wanted us to find them, to read them. To know something about you through them—somehow. The way they vanished is as much a part of their story as having them would have been.

I can only recall in flashes: I remember the notebook paper on which you had typed the "Dear Charles" missive: the precision of the ink black raven and the intensity of the cerulean blue colored pencil drawing at the bottom of the page. The first line: "Charles, you fucking bastard ..." I knew there was no Charles, but that this was a rant to an internal foe. I remember the red ink of "My Failed Engagement"—about a half-page of your handwriting. I would be curious to read any thoughts you had written about that event.

I remember my hunger for your words. I remember pre-relishing how I would feel when I took the time to read and absorb these words you had purposely left for us. I knew I would ache over them. I knew I would marvel over them. I knew I would want to wrap my arms around you and hear more—and reassure you that you did not need to be so scathingly hard on yourself. And ... I remember leaving them in your room. To relish later—when I could sink into them ... and into the horror of your absence. Stacked just so.

And then police things happened. Coroner things happened. When I next entered your room, the pages had vanished. More than once, I have walked through those agonizing first moments: falling on the icy sidewalk in my rush to get to you; your blood on J's coat; regulating my breathing and focusing on her trauma; knowing you were in the backyard, knowing I would not be allowed to see you, knowing I could have insisted and been able to see you, to hold you (DON'T YOU FUCKING TOUCH HIM! I BROUGHT HIM INTO THIS WORLD AND I WANT TO HOLD HIM.) But coroners have their jobs, the police have theirs. And those jobs were being done. I stayed in front, while you were in back.

I did not think about blood—your blood. I did not think about brain matter—your brain matter. I did not think about the brightness of blood on the whiteness of snow. I did not think about the gun. So close to your hand that it had to have been your hand that had held it. Your finger that squeezed the trigger.

Am I relieved now that this scene and these details exist only in my imagination? Am I relieved that the utter devastation of the actual scene of your violent death is not seared into my visual cortex? I suppose I have to say, "Yes." However, I was troubled by the assertions of those who said, "You can't change what happened, so why haunt yourself with the memories?" It did not help me to hear it is better that I did not see him. It did not help me to hear that the coroner had a job to do.

There are moments when we are Ground Zero. I did not need to be removed from the horror of my son's death. I did

102

not need to be protected from it. I needed to be with him.

Now—of course—I am forming an understanding about just how traumatic it could have been for me to see Tanner's dead body and his blood on site. My imagination's images haunt me plenty. My heart and soul and my momma's arms want to think I would have brought a wisdom, a courage, and my keening grief to the moments shared with his body in all of its horrible rawness that would have—somehow—shazammed me into understanding. I did not need the horror of it; I needed the beauty of him. I did not need the shock of his death; I needed the brutal beauty of our connection. In some moments we are Ground Zero. It's not that I think I could have shared that moment with him—because of course he was gone—and somehow lessened his pain. It's that the loss of him—and the absolute heart-crushing absence of him—made me want to sit at Ground Zero. To say, the world has swallowed up my boy. And it is the awfullest of awful things. And I need to sit here. I will sit here. On this spot. With him. To bear witness.

I felt him there. I knew he was with us. And all I wanted was to be with him.

And the phantom pages? They've never surfaced. The cops don't have them. The coroner doesn't have them. They've never materialized among Tanner's things. I still think J took them and doesn't want to cop to that. I also know I was out of my mind that night. I've walked myself through all the minutes that I recall of that night, and the pages are not part of my memory after I left T's room. J did bring the topic of the pages up not very long ago, asking if I had checked with the police again about them. Part of me wondered if she feels guilty about taking them and can't admit it. I visited the police again. They—again—showed me pictures they had taken of T's note and the two checks he left out. No pages. Mysterious.

Traumatic stress responses happen more than we talk about, and triggers within the home or other environments are common. The first step in recovery of traumatic stress responses is increasing your awareness surrounding them.

Some people find that when they next enter a hospital they experience a panic attack or a sense of overwhelm, of having to leave. If you get to the point of understanding: *Oh yes, of course that might happen; this is a normal response to something that felt so very abnormal and traumatic, and at some level my mind-body was reminded of that,* you can then work on ways to calm and prepare yourself for a similar situation in the future.

Of course these responses may feel overwhelming in the moment. But try doing the earlier-mentioned even breath-work to bring your sympathetic drive or fight/flight response down. And, as soon as you are grounded enough, mentally filter through what may have been your trigger.

With traumatic stress responses, knowledge is the power that deflates the balloon of stress and allows you eventually to understand and be better prepared for situations that might prove difficult.

As mentioned before, EMDR is an excellent form of therapy with relatively quick results, if you find you need some gentle assistance to help you through those responses of high activation of your traumatic grief.

With regard to traditional therapy and grief counseling, you can't expect to report your deep traumatic feelings to a "professional" whose experiential scope has never touched that place and have them really understand.

Let me say it again: What precipitates trauma, how it feels, what it looks like, is individual to each person.

Reminder: it is okay (no, imperative) to ask if the professional you seek therapy from has experienced deep loss themselves. That is a criterion I would recommend for those professionals doing therapy or counseling with the bereaved. Admittedly, deep loss brings many counselors and therapists to that practice. Within the grief support section at the end of this book you will find some of those people who have special training *and* have experienced deep grief themselves. In our changing times, many of them will do video sessions if you are not in their geographic area.

For comparison with a helper who hasn't experienced deep grief, imagine a man patting a woman's head during the throes of intense labor and telling her how the physical sensations she is having *should* be feeling. *That*. It doesn't mean such people are the devil—it's simply that they are unable to understand deeply until they've been there.

It brings me back to my young nursing days. There was a labor and delivery nurse who could be so very rude to laboring moms—*stop whining; quiet down; stop being a baby*. It was disgusting.

And then what happened? She had a baby herself. I happened to observe her in labor and delivery after that, and guess what? She exhibited the kindest and most understanding bedside manner.

Before? *She just did not get it.* She had not one clue about the intensity of these women's experiences.

A few years ago, I was visiting the US and had lunch with an old friend who was previously my clinical and actual supervisor. She'd had an onslaught of deep loss from death since I'd last seen her. At one point she leaned over the table and said, almost whispering, "What were we doing with our grieving clients before we'd gone through this? I want to go back and apologize. I want to say, I'm sorry, I just didn't know."

take-me-with-you, grief

These are words that people frequently keep tightly closeted, not trusting their own recurring thoughts, fearing that people will question their sanity, while they are questioning their own.

First and foremost, please understand that these can be common thoughts and feelings in the early days of grief.

This seems more common in parents who have had a child die, or a partner, but can surface from the death of anyone perceived as a deep connection, especially if the deceased was part of their day-to-day living.

One thing you find, when you create a space where people can share their experience with you, is that people may have patterns of thinking in which their imagination runs with a wide spectrum of scenarios. When people are experiencing a heart-wrenching emotional process they never understood possible, it isn't unusual for them to think—*I just want to be with my loved one.*

That happens frequently enough that we needed to mention it here. This is an important fact for support people to understand, as well as the griever.

It can be a normal reaction.

Typically, this type of thinking has a relatively short phase and moves through. Being able to openly express these thoughts and feelings, without judgment, can feel supportive.

Of course, the concern lies when thoughts of wanting to join a dead loved one are persistent and gather intensity.

One question it is okay to ask your person or yourself is: *Have you actually thought about following through with those thoughts?*

It is one thing to have thoughts like, *I just want to be with my baby and hold my baby.* Or: *I can't wait to die and be reunited,* while still feeling one's feet firmly on the planet.

Thoughts like: *I can't stay on the planet and need to go be with my loved ones,* along with speculating how you might do that, suggest that immediate intervention is warranted. Get in to see a trusted medical or mental health professional and share your thoughts. They will understand. They will have heard such thoughts before. You are not alone.

If you are a support person, it's okay to wade into those difficult questions or conversations. If this has been an invasive thought for a grieving person, there may be relief for them in knowing they can be heard and understood. It's like the survivor who says: *Why do people think they can't say their name? I'm thinking about them all the time anyway.*

When I first began conducting suicide assessments in my work, it felt very uncomfortable to forge ahead with that line of questioning. But after observing the person breathe out and openly respond, time after time, I quickly realized the vast majority of people who are having thoughts of ending their lives feel a visceral exhale when the door is opened for them to share those intrusive thoughts. Learning they are experiencing *symptom thinking* rather than thoughts based in reality can be greatly liberating.

This is not an area for you to take on alone, however. Reassuring your person that what they are experiencing is not unusual, and then helping them schedule an appointment with their physician or a mental health professional, is an act of love.

My recommendation has always been to be *proactive instead of reactive* with seeking intervention. Don't wait until you may be experiencing a crisis point to find a trusted, trained person you can interact with. As so many of our interviews have suggested, getting immediate assistance from a professional after your person dies is highly recommended.

It's the smart person who seeks help.

Don't buy into stigma-based lies society feeds us. Our brain is an organ of our body, and it, and our tender hearts, require extra care during these times when our mind can become filled with distorted thinking in reaction to trauma.

relieved grief

Sometimes the circumstances of a person's living lead to feeling a palpable exhale when they die.

Maybe their suffering has ended.

Maybe their frustration at searching for viable treatments may now be over.

Maybe *this* attempt at taking their life succeeded.

We shall refrain from running down the varying scenarios, because you will know very well if you can relate to the term *relieved grief* and may have been hiding away with guilt.

Please understand that you are not evil if you experienced an audible exhale when your loved one took leave. Some people understand that; others will find themselves guilt-ridden—tortured—by

107

their *relief*.

And don't be surprised for a moment if a stronger form of grief circles back around on you at some point.

Sometimes, relieved grief comes from extended illness and exhaustion, but other times it comes when the person had been mired in addiction and/or involved in risk-taking behaviors, when every phone call or knock on the door was met with fear that it would announce their death. Maybe there were repeated overdoses, which left the griever feeling as if their loved one had already died a thousand deaths.

Feeling relief doesn't mean you didn't care. It is simply the exhale that occurs when you've been holding your breath for so long you didn't even realize you were teetering around hypoxic. You'd become used to walking around oxygen-deprived, with a lingering sense of dread and even hopelessness that you may not have fully recognized.

Feeling relief doesn't mean you loved that person any less; it means their suffering was torturing you, just as you worried it was torturing them.

Feeling relief may be birthed from love and care for the departed and those who loved them.

That type of feeling may complicate your aftermath if you feel guilt about such a reaction. Acknowledge your feelings and thoughts about the circumstances. Acknowledge your humanness, and let go of guilt as best you can.

This is another of those times when there are no brilliant words that make everything better. But it is my wish that, by understanding that your experience of relieved grief is not unique to you and that many others have walked that path, you may give yourself a sense of grace and step away from self-deprecation.

As I re-read the above words, written before my brother was recently found dead, I felt a full-body exhale, almost thanking myself for providing this feedback. As I mentioned earlier, I did feel a sense of release for him after his death, and I have to imagine that my writing on this topic was a bit of foreshadowing. It certainly paved the way for being at least somewhat prepared for that phone call we all dread receiving.

I can't know for absolute certain, but I want to believe that it was being so immersed in these concepts and conversations and stories that helped ease the grief transition after a death that I feared would have shattered me.

May you understand that feeling a sense of relief or release after a loved one's death does not negate your love or loyalty to that person, but rather signals the layers of circumstance that lay beneath this death.

it's complicated

How grief shows up when it involves someone with whom you've had a complicated relationship isn't often discussed. Nor are the complexities of experiencing multiple losses in a brief period.

My father's death brought a complex grief. He raised his children as an intimidating, sometimes violent, mostly rage-filled presence. With the general public, at work and at church, he was a kind, funny, helpful person. I saw the father he could have been any time we were out of our home and in how he treated my friends.

Inside our home, I lived in fear and remained hyper-vigilant, always waiting for the next unpredictable outburst.

At the time he died from a ruptured brain aneurysm, we gathered in his room as he was taken off life support. Our family was divinely bestowed with grace and compassion during that daylong vigil in the neurological ICU. In fact, nurses who witnessed his death with us embraced us, saying they'd never seen so much love in a room. I'm quite certain that love, showing up as it did, surprised us all.

Afterwards, even though there was a palpable sense of relief that my mother would frequently verbalize, now that she no longer lived in constant fear, I was baffled by the layers of complex feelings I had surrounding his demise.

I had been out of the home for four years by then, but the stress of being around my father never lessened. Even though he generally was on his best behavior in our presence after we became adults and left our family home, there was a time when I was twenty that he'd backhanded me in the car on the way to a family reunion. A safe place, he was not.

It did not take long for me to realize that I was not so much mourning the father I had lived with for my first eighteen years of life, and been terrified of and terrorized by, as I was mourning his public face, which had always shown me the kind of father he *could* have been. I was mourning the father that I had always longed to see show up. The fathering he failed to provide us. The kindness he always showed others but could not muster for his own children and wife.

My brother who recently died was, of the four children, the one who bore the brunt of my father's actions into his adulthood.

Our family always held a gentle understanding of that fact in our hearts. We were able to see that brother's endearing qualities dancing with his less-than-functional ways of coping, all the while knowing about the mistreated little guy who lived inside him. There was a deep sadness that our childhood had landed him in a situation of discontent where he remained for the majority of his life. Living was so very hard for him.

So many ambivalent feelings.

Love, anger, care, disgust, never-ending hope that one day he'd get the help he needed to live more peacefully and gently with himself and others.

The feelings surrounding my brother were very complicated when he was alive, so of course they are going to be the ingredients for a complicated, complex grief process. I am thankful, as I've mentioned earlier, to realize how much I had been processing that grief actively over the five years prior to his death.

Many of us are experts on complicated or complex grief, although we may not know it. Why? Because our lives, our relationships, are so very complex. Such is the nature of life.

Unfortunately, the little generic bites we are spoon-fed about grief are usually of the one-size-fits-all variety, so people frequently feel *less than*, or believe they must be damaged, when their loss brings out so many varied reactions. Feeling abnormal becomes fertile ground for stuffing or hiding or denying our many and varied emotions about a death.

Within such a complicated aftermath, we might see a variety of things creeping in: depression, stress intolerance, traumatic stress, anxiety, or flat-out emotional fatigue. And as Madeleine expressed in her interview about Mahyan, "It's been my work, with the help of people, to uncover what it looks like to show up kindly to a body that has been broken by grief."

I, too, have experienced a body broken by grief. Maybe you have as well.

Although there has been progress, we still don't have a medical system that fully appreciates how stress affects our body's functioning. You'd think that, with all the research done, for example, on a known entity like broken-heart syndrome, when our bodies are breaking down, inquiries would begin with probing our emotional health.

My primary point is to understand that grief is not always straightforward. Be open to the many layers of complexities yours may hold.

Remember to be kind to yourself.

Consider writing out your feelings. Maybe as letters to your loved ones who have passed. Maybe as letters to yourself from them.

Many find writing mourning pages (a take on the traditional morning page practice) helpful. Before you arise and start your day, grab your journal and free-write.

No censor, no processing, no planning—simply let the words flow out of your pen or fingertips. Some people go for a thousand words. Give it some time. Try at least fifteen to thirty minutes.

This can be a very cleansing way to start your day, and you will see the "aha" moments float up. Things you hadn't previously put together will start to surface.

But if you have to start with something as simple as *I don't like waking up this early, I feel my fingers on the keyboard,* roll with that. No one will read it. It's a practice of giving yourself permission to let what's inside out. And it takes *practice*. Going through the motions.

You may also find yourself remembering dreams during this process.

Some say that this practice in those first waking moments begins to feel like a sacred time.

Whatever your belief system, many people who never considered themselves the writing type have found great comfort in this practice.

Naturally, you may find that you need some assistance from a professional, or at least the very wise ear of someone who has had a similar experience, to sort through layers of complex grieving. That's a smart choice.

Again, make sure any professional you choose is someone who has experienced deep loss; it's okay to interview them prior to making an appointment so you can have a sense of whether you will connect.

The very first step during any acute loss is to not lose sight of what our mind-body-spirit needs.

Remember to return to the basics: Nourish yourself. Stay hydrated. Rest your weary bones.

Refrain from being overly self-critical, bringing yourself back into the present moment if you become overwhelmed with judgments and what-ifs.

Try to ground yourself into what the new *now* feels like for you.

Encourage yourself to gravitate to those healthy practices you have previously found nurturing.

May you go gently, gently, ever so gently, and give yourself time.

losing someone who lives in your home: they are everywhere & nowhere

Years ago, I sat across from someone who came to see me because of their toddler's death. Decades later, their words still echo: *On this particular day, I was doing "okay" but then I pulled the couch out to clean underneath it, and there was her pacifier. I fell to the ground.*

Hearing this recollection was almost a remembering within my cells.

Of course.

Of course this happens, and especially in the case of the death of a child. Of course, you will be finding pieces of them left in the nooks and crannies, where they had last touched an item. And of course that would bring one to their knees.

But experientially? I didn't fully understand that experience until my mother's death, after she lived with us for two years.

I just want to name this experience for you in case you find yourself in it in the future.

My father died when I was 22 and had long been out of their home. Yes, there was a complex grief that accompanied the aftermath of his death.

My brother's death had unhinged me.

But nine months later, the experience of having had my mother living with us brought something different to my family's grief.

Of course there are the logistics—what to do with their belongings; the busy-ness that might come with having someone within your household die. But for me, there was something that touched me deeper and was longer lasting.

Walking by my mother's room nearing four years later, I still smell the scent of her when the door has been closed and I open it. I reckon that will always be *her* room.

Part of me expects to see my mom in her rocking chair when I walk by her room, coyly smiling as she peeks up from writing in her journal.

If I'm outside and glance up at the large window that faces out to our front view, I expect to see her smiling and waving, as she always did.

Her seat in the living room—the only one she sat in—seemed to still hold her presence, and, at a glance, I would expect to see her there.

For months, every time we went grocery shopping, the thought popped into our heads—*Wonder what Mom would like for a treat?*—before remembering the current reality. On the way home, we'd wonder if she'd be napping when we returned. She had become such a part of our everyday life, an integral part of the rhythm of our days. The void her exit left was accentuated far more than if we hadn't been living together.

This section is written just to say, if you've lost someone within your home setting, *I see you.*

I understand the challenges.

I fully know how a part of your person still lingers all around you, and you may find yourself searching for signs of them. And yes, some people might want to barricade their rooms or any trace of them because they find it too painful to deal with, for the time being.

Our minds can perform bizarre acrobatics while we are acutely grieving.

Buckle in. This one is raw and bizarre. We live in the country and are on a septic system for our waste. Every few years, you call the guy who pulls up in a big truck and puts something down into the tank that vacuums the waste out. The first time that happened after my brother and mom died, I had a sense of panic. There were remnants of both of them in that septic tank, and they were going to vanish. I mean, *what the actual hell?* Where did that come from? And I had to go to the extreme of appeasing myself by thinking that there's still a hint of part of who they were when they were alive in there. I mean, talk about bizarre, magical thinking! Brought to you by your mental health specialist.

Yes, I was able to talk myself down, but hey-ho, what a strange trip it's been.

And I allow myself to share this wonky side of my experience because of all the people I've spoken with telling me their wonky experiences. Grief will have its way with you, and at times that way feels bizarre.

And other times, a thought of them in your environment may feel deeply comforting. Or bring you to your knees, depending on your current emotional climate.

You may feel their presence.

You may hear their voice.

You may see them out of the corner of your eye.

Their clothes turning up in the laundry, or finding that lost item, may dismantle you months down the line.

Recently a guest was staying in my mom's room and, from outside, I glanced up at the glass wall that opens to the front of our house, and she was holding my mom's white slippers that she'd found under the dresser. It almost seemed like there was a smug, *what's this?* look on her face.

"Yep," I said, "Those are my mom's, I keep them there. You can put them back."

Call it bizarre if you must, but I *like* the thought of her slippers being in the room where she lived and died, hidden from view.

I had donated much of my mother's clothing just after her death. There were shirts she had worn in my childhood. Those remain. A shirt of hers remains hanging in the laundry room. I don't do well with the idea that every trace of the person's existence disappears immediately after their death—or, in my case, years after.

Each to their own.

You do you when it comes to handling the environment after your loved one's death. There is no right or wrong way.

Occasionally, we hear of or see portrayals where veritable shrines have been erected in homes. Recently someone told me how they had done so. And there came a time it just didn't feel right anymore, and memorabilia was slowly, methodically dismantled.

When my children were small, I remember the gentle child-rearing expert, T. Berry Brazelton's response to people's angst over the tardiness of their child giving up their pacifier or being out of diapers. He would always comment in his gentle way, something to the effect of: *Let it go. We don't see many first graders walking around in diapers, with their pacifiers.* And he'd frequently retort in response to inquiries, *Whose problem is it? The child's? Or yours?* Inevitably, it was the adult's.

Keep in mind that some of your grief responses may make other people uncomfortable. Ask yourself: *Whose problem is it?*

People communicate many directives to grievers because of their own discomfort with being in the presence of such deep complexities. Of course they'd feel better if we just got on with it. You will, but in your own unique way.

Sometimes your space holds the remnants of trauma from finding your deceased loved one or memories of their dying process. Refer back to traumatic grief and tread gently with yourself.

May you experience the memories surrounding you, in the places you shared with your loved one, moving into an overwhelming feeling of love and gratitude for what you shared there.

who-am-I-now grief

When the death we've experienced creates a change in our life's job description, we can find ourselves not only mourning our person/people but also mourning the person we previously identified as: partner, parent, child, sibling, to name a few.

I hear from people who speak of the first time they ticked the *widowed* box and were mind-blown that their entire identity had changed. The structure of their days, their social structure, their family structure, their views into the future are dismantled.

Some people report being stuck in that limbo, searching for the way out, but feel the reactions from the world around them do little to facilitate their escape or to enhance reestablishing their identity while honoring who they were with their person.

Invitations and connection with other couples dwindle off.

116

Some people claim they feel like a pariah. Many surmise their friends have a fear of sidling too close to death that fuels the disconnection.

It may be the case that the widowed survivor symbolizes the walk couples know they will eventually take too and long to remain in denial about.

To be fair, some invitations stop because people don't want to put *you* in an uncomfortable position. All these reasons lie just under the surface, because of the cultural norms of not speaking openly and asking each other what would feel best.

Please, have the conversations.

Grievers, share your needs with your people.

People, ask what your grieving person would like, *needs*, all the while understanding the moving target of grief's impact on another.

When an infant or child dies, an immense part of our identity and structure of our living dies.

And with the death of parents and siblings, depending on what developmental stage of life you are in, your entire day-to-day way of life may come down like a teetering tower of blocks, as the very structure your being was built upon suddenly feels wobbly.

When a part of our intimate circle departs the planet, a gap is left. A gap that will never be filled. Eventually the rest of our life compensates so the circle isn't as warped and debilitated forever, but the gap is only ever thinly veiled, and now, that person's absence is also a part of our identity, much as their presence in our life was.

Yet still, most humans skip around these facts and opportunities to discuss the parts of our lives that have the most impact, the most *real* parts of our lives.

When we eventually form our new way of walking in the world, it is because we let something meaningful grow in the gap we were left with. This may take years, but one day you may find that your experience, and the love you shared with your loved one, has nurtured new, meaningful growth in your life.

That is one way they remain with you always.

I frequently say that grief dismantled me and put me back

together differently. It did. And you are reading part of how it put me back together. This project was a choice I made as to what I wanted to do with death and grief.

I believe deep loss changes us on a cellular level. And if we are aware of that concept and are open to change, rather than fighting it, we may find a transformation that we'd never expected.

What I know for sure is that after grief has totally dismantled you, there will be a day when that bell rings, if you are listening, signaling the moment of considering: *What do I want to include in the rest of my life?* And the answer becomes a direction you can choose to walk towards.

May you understand the normality of feeling dismantled by grief and gently await the time when you are ready to willingly explore what you'd like your life, *after*, to hold.

please-don't-let-anyone-else-die grief

I've spoken with parents who have had children die and tell of a reaction that follows them: unspoken fear.

They've seen that what was once previously unimaginable can happen, and they find a fear of losing another child, or anyone, follows them.

And while they want to convince themselves that, statistically, that won't happen, they have seen that sometimes it does happen. Such as my friend, who experienced the sudden unexpected, and unrelated, deaths of her two young-adult children within six weeks.

Our family's experience with rapid-fire death had me experiencing the *please no more* grief.

We all know of examples that have shown us that death isn't always compassionate in its choices. Some would say death is never kind.

We may find ways to acknowledge those thoughts and fears of future deaths.

Let us understand that it is grief having its wily way with us and make the choice to put our energy into those relationships we are so fearful will leave us.

Let us work at staying in each and every moment and decidedly handing those thoughts an eviction notice from our brain.

Death *will* visit again—our own or someone else's. This we know. What we do not know is how or why or when.

Every minute that we find ourselves speculating about those fears, gazing into a nonexistent crystal ball, takes us away from living our life in that very moment.

May you understand how perfectly normal it is that death's visit has triggered a fear or concern in you about when it will again knock on your door.

no-one-ever-told-me-it-would-hurt-this-bad grief

Actually, this sentiment accounts for almost every person I have spoken with who has had a significant person in their life die.

Let me be very clear. There is no front-loading that gives you a *get out of grief free* card, although many of us have thought our deep inner work would have afforded us this luxury.

Recall my conversation with a former colleague who was embarrassed that we actually sat with people in therapy and tried to *help* them before experiencing our own great loss. Exposure to others' stories helps our understanding, but until you feel your own great loss, you do not learn that deep and mysterious thing that can never be taught.

The uniqueness of every human, every death, every situation, every setting, every other human in that orbit, every emotion, every bit of history, everything, it all forms a foundation for an unpredictable experience.

But just like when we are transitioning a soul into this life, if we can unclench and not brace against the discomfort—if we can release and expand and feel all the feelings that come with the experience— we have the potential to open up to a bigger and broader way of being

119

in the world than we ever knew was possible. And that, too, will look different for every person.

This is what I call *full-spectrum living.*

In full-spectrum living, we open to the beautiful *and* the horrible. We understand that during this transitional period, we don't have to have all of the correct answers; we simply must be in the moment and experience all that love and death is bringing to us.

We can embrace the idea that within this unimaginable pain lie magical lessons that we will take into the deaths we experience in the future, be it our own or others.

As outlined before, those early days of sitting with the unimaginable are the days to cocoon in self-care. Please revisit the sections *help me now* and *traumatic grief* and the next section, *I can't get you off my mind,* for some concrete suggestions. The golden thread woven through all these words is that what you are feeling is quite normal and expected; let that be the raft that holds you above the waters in those early days as you acclimatize to the temperature of your new life. Eventually you will find you can swim more freely in that new ocean of your tomorrows.

May your grief move through you gently as you feel yourself tugged and pulled and shaped into a more expansive and understanding version of yourself, eyes and heart wide open to the beautiful–horrible of your living and the full knowledge that death *will* visit again.

I can't get you off my mind

Going out on a limb, I will declare that this is a universal happening for people who have experienced great loss; yet, again, it is something we have not openly discussed.

Most people I have spoken with report a period of time after a death when they find that thoughts of the deceased person or circumstances surrounding their death are constantly on their minds. There may be flashbacks or replays, much like we discussed with regard to traumatic grief—almost as if there is a fear that if they don't keep actively remembering, they might forget them.

Therefore there is a faction of the grieving in society who are questioning their sanity because they are constantly thinking about their deceased loved one.

Maybe they are reliving the scenes surrounding the death, as we discussed in the section on traumatic grief.

For some time, they were my first thought when I awakened in the morning: my mom and brother. And throughout the day. And as I went to sleep at night. And if I had to get up in the middle of the night.

My personal remedy was to send them love each time and return to the breathing pattern previously outlined in the *help me now* section.

Riding on love has been the only thing that has gotten me through the incessant missing of my loved ones, resting my overworking brain, which seemed to be trying to *think* them back to life.

I don't want to pathologize a normal developmental stage of grief many of us go through after loss, but with the prevalence of anxiety in humans, this conversation needs to be expanded, because for some people this develops into more than a stage of their grief.

The primary symptom of generalized anxiety is *overthinking* or *worrying*.

Having observed generations of my family live their entire lives with anxiety symptoms, the possibility of a genetic predisposition is not lost on me. Most saw it as part of their personality, as generations before them had. Ever hear the term *worry wart?* That, my friend, would most likely be someone with anxiety.

Part of my *therapist gone rogue* shtick stems from many years of having to diagnose people from the lists in the Diagnostic and Statistics Manual of mental disorders (DSM). I am now at a stage of life where I'm much more interested in meeting people just where they are, and fully hearing their stories, without them being identified as a diagnosis.

That said, self-awareness is essential to our overall optimal functioning. What many people, even in the mental health fields, do not realize is the physiological component to anxiety.

Let me share the simplified basics with you.

Our autonomic nervous system (ANS) is composed of the sympathetic (fight-flight-freeze) and parasympathetic drive (balance/relax). Some people's ANS baseline happens to run a bit more in the sympathetically driven lane, the *flight or fight* action of our mind–body. That rev we feel when an animal darts out in front of us when we are driving or we see the police lights in our rear-view mirror. That response you experience in your mind–body is a concrete example of the sympathetic drive at work.

In everyday life, it may take on many faces: sleep difficulties, gut issues, nervousness, irritability, worry, panic attacks, tension, migraines and heart pounding, to name a few.

Even so, I've worked with many a person whose exterior presented as zen, but their ANS balance, as indicated by measuring their HRV (heart rate variability) with technology, suggested someone with an overactive sympathetic drive. So the idea that we can tell a person's level of nervousness or inner restlessness by the way they present just isn't accurate.

We can be born with a higher-revving sympathetic drive—I call this being set on *high idle*. Just like with a car, you can imagine its engine revving (sympathetically driven) or just humming along (balanced ANS) or ticking away so slowly that it is barely puttering (parasympathetically driven).

Finally, research has surfaced, as I knew it eventually would, showing that those newborn temperaments we learned about in our Psych 101 classes are correlated with where our physiological set-point is within our ANS.

The more sympathetically driven babes are more hyper-alert, may have sleep difficulties, possess a heightened startle reflex and can seem discontented, difficult to soothe.

The mid-range babies are just that—they are okay sleepers; they fuss sometimes but are easy enough to soothe; average.

And the low idle, or more parasympathetically driven babes, are the ones who are consistently chill. You lay them down and they go to sleep. They wake up cooing or giggling or chattering. Their startle isn't extreme. What we would call a very *easy* baby. Until you witness one, it's difficult to believe they exist. You *know* there is a reason when they cry.

My eldest granddaughter was a low-idle baby, and I was fascinated observing this aspect of her. I have a video of my daughter clapping loudly in front of her as an infant. She squints her eyes and then smiles with each startling clap. If that had been her mother, as a higher-idle infant, she would have shivered and cried with that startle. We are all so very different.

The higher-idle person, through no fault of their own, will tend more toward experiencing an inability to shut their thinking down; they may have a propensity towards anxiety attacks, sleep problems, muscle tension, gut issues, and other stress-related symptoms, as mentioned earlier. It bears noting that these symptoms, when running rampant, are the perfect recipe for depression. When the incessant thinking is negative or self-deprecating, and the mind–body isn't given time or space for rejuvenation and calming regulation, depressive symptoms may spiral out of control. Rarely does one see a clinical depression unaccompanied by those high-sympathetic-drive effects.

Also, we need to consider that an average or low-idle baby can turn into a high-idle person if they are raised in a stressful environment or exposed to trauma.

Imagine soldiers in foxholes during wartime active duty. Of course your ANS will go into overdrive when you have to stay hyper-vigilant to keep yourself safe, while witnessing the traumas of war. Sometimes it gets stuck in the high-idle space—either extremely, as is the case with PTSD, or just never quite getting back down into the lower idle/more parasympathetic balance where they started life.

Why this little lesson? Because I believe it is an irresponsible lie that we have been teaching people, having them think their anxiety is a mental illness that is all in their head, when it has a physiological foundation.

If you were born with an ANS that is more sympathetically

driven or lived in an environment that taught your system to be hyper-vigilant, you are probably experiencing anxiety-type symptoms as part of your grief process.

The good news is, you can practice ANS balancing techniques, and if you do so regularly, you can actually lower your idle into the mid-range and keep it there with ongoing practice.

In my therapy practice, I used these techniques with clients who were so high-idle that they were having daily panic attacks, and with regular practice, within a week or so, they were not having *any* panic attacks. I also conducted a study with 150 people and saw the benefits that ANS balancing techniques had on mind–body health.

The caveat? One must practice the techniques regularly.

What I want you to take away from this conversation is that if your thoughts of your loved one have an intrusive or obsessive quality, that's perfectly normal, and there are things you can do to ease that occurrence.

And no, it will not destroy your ability to think about your loved one.

You will simply think about them when you want to, or when they occasionally pop into your mind.

And if it's deeper connection you desire with them in the afterlife, all recommendations point to the need to be centered for such contact. These steps move you closer to being able to have access to that type of groundedness.

Your sympathetic drive will no longer be driving the car and playing records—on repeat—in your brain. First, they will move into the passenger seat, and eventually to the back seat. But again, don't worry; you'll be able to see them in your rear-view mirror, when you want, instead of them grabbing the steering wheel and veering you off-road.

Let's revisit the technique outlined in the section *help me now* and review that conversation about the breath-work technique. That is your ANS balancing superpower.

Breathing in and out, to the count of five or six or whatever is comfortable, but keeping the breath regular.

Imagine with each inhale that you are breathing love into your heart area from your loved one, and on exhale you are breathing love out of your heart area, to your loved one. Stay with *feeling* rather than *thoughts*. If that isn't possible, create an emotionally positive thought that is relevant for you. *I am calm and relaxed. All is well. Love lives on.* For medicinal purposes, with troubling symptoms like incessant worry, obsessive thoughts, sleep issues, panic/anxiety disorders, routinely do this technique for ten minutes prior to rising after you awaken and for another ten minutes as you go to sleep at night. This is your baseline medicine, and it's more effectively practiced at those times when your ANS is at its most naturally balanced.

Just like when we stop taking our antibiotics after three days instead of continuing for the full ten, this practice is prone to what I call the *antibiotic effect*. Many folks with extreme clinical anxiety have practiced it, raved about their cure, and then stopped using it because, um, *cured*. And *boom*. The symptoms returned. So yes, regular practice is most effective for transformational results.

And then, use it here and there throughout your day. Certainly if you are moving into a stressful zone or if troubling thoughts or immense waves of grief arise.

Also, I use it just to ground or recenter all day, throughout my day. Maybe just a few breaths at a time, but your mind–body will soon become conditioned with regular practice. When I do this practice, my ANS regulates and I experience the benefits of that balance.

If you are experiencing sleep difficulties, continue the practice at bedtime with lights out, but for sleep, count backwards from 100 with each breath. Don't wait until you know you are having a sleepless night before you do this. If you practice this on less difficult nights, your mind–body will quickly learn: *When I do this breath-work while counting backwards with each breath, I go to sleep.* It's a bit of a self-hypnosis practice. People find this very effective. But again, you have to do it *regularly* for it to work. Trying it once or twice and declaring it unsuccessful isn't giving the practice the time it needs. Depending on how fired-up your

125

ANS is, it can take a while before your mind–body responds to the regulation techniques, but with continued effort it won't take long.

May you understand that many of your troubling symptoms can have a physiological base, and may you find the energy and motivation to begin the regulation practice that will ease your overthinking mind.

regret: shoulda, coulda, woulda

It is appropriate to read about this topic after reading the previous one, because they may be closely entwined.

One common aspect of thinking that accompanies grief is regret.

This regret can be related to aspects of the distant and not-so-distant past; how you behaved with the person throughout their life or at the end of their life; choices you made or did not make surrounding their death. You get it—the list of possibilities is endless.

My friend, I'm not here to tell you that what you are thinking or feeling is not valid, but one thing I know is true: every single day of our lives, we could have done or said or chosen something differently that would have made someone else's or our own experience a bit more gentle.

Know that this issue doesn't exist only in relation to your departed loved one. That is simply where it screams out to you, because you feel you no longer have the ability to make this right with your person.

I personally bow at the feet of the great mystery. But whatever your belief system is, maybe you can wrap your head around the idea that it's okay to continue to have conversations with your deceased loved ones.

Maybe these can take place in your journal, or out loud on your walks outside, or in your car. With the prevalence of people talking in public on their bluetooth devices to an unseen listener, I no longer care who sees me chatting it up with the dead.

Those conversations are one safe place to lay down your regrets.

Consider treating *yourself* like you would a dear friend—soften.

Invite grace. Look at the situation objectively, rather than through your guilt-colored glasses.

Consider that over-focusing on these regrets may be distracting you from recognizing underlying deeper feelings and, in that way, may serve the purpose of letting you simmer for a bit before you dig further into what lies beneath.

Consider love.

Did your person know that they were loved and cared for?

And for the person who is new to this terrain or just walking into the moments of dying with someone, when you are doubting what to do, let this overarching question be your guide: *Will I regret doing or not doing this later?*

One person whose partner had an extended illness mentioned that her kids were starting to worry whether they were spending enough time with the ailing parent, because, of course, life was moving on for them and there were places to go, and people to see, and the unpredictability of what the time-frame was that their family was looking at with their loved one. I encouraged them to suggest to the kids that they check in with themselves when they were stuck: *If this parent dies, will I have regrets about this decision?*

We need to remind ourselves: there would never have been enough time; there were never enough visits; there will always be conversations we wish we'd had; there will be questions left unanswered; there will be things we could have done better.

May we embrace our "enoughness" and refrain from repeatedly second-guessing our experiences with our deceased loved one, gently reminding ourselves not to let regret smother our undying love.

secondary loss and grief

Another aspect of grief for which most people find themselves totally unprepared is the secondary losses that occur after the death of a primary person in their lives.

It can feel like a cruel joke when we notice there are people retreating from our lives after experiencing profound loss: the parents

127

we associated with, other couples, friends who feel ill-equipped to be present, people who run from death.

Maybe you sense you are being approached less within your workplace or overlooked when exciting challenges come up because people may be concerned about adding undue stress. Rarely are those actions, or lack thereof, spoken of transparently, nor is the person included in the decision-making.

Hopefully workplaces are becoming more grief-literate, taking their blinders off and having open discussions with their employees when they return to work. The fact that employees who feel their experience is validated and honored will perform better seems a no-brainer.

When our parent status or couple status changes, we can find our existence redefined. Not fitting into the spaces we used to be part of heaps more loss upon the already painful loss. A constant reminder that things will never be quite the same.

Peer groups, socializing, and support structures may change or vanish, reminding us we are forever changed.

There may be upheaval in the income stream, changing the way you live and move forward. Throughout all of the stories of loss, a common thread is that subsequent losses are an unspoken factor that greatly complicates lives in the aftermath of a loved one's death. The unspoken-ness of it all can be as frustrating and invalidating as that secondary loss itself.

There is no magic wand to prevent such losses nor ameliorate them, but as with so many other areas of life post-loss, you might find it a wee bit helpful to understand that this is a universal issue.

You are not alone.

Most of the healing that occurs when it comes to secondary loss involves connecting with others who have had a similar experience and can relate to your situation. Experiencing the understanding of others and realizing you are not alone can indeed be a healing balm.

As you feel able, consider being proactive and speaking with your employer and work mates, groups you are involved with, social

128

groups, etc., having an honest discussion of your hopes and how you'd like to be treated.

No, it isn't fair for you to have to do all the work, and hopefully people will arise and share that burden with you. But if you view it as self-care, versus clearing up someone's lack of ability to show up, that may help you find the energy to advocate for yourself.

Again, deep loss is dismantling. As you put yourself back together, try to keep what's in the best interest of your well-being in the forefront—with the choices you make, the people you choose to have in your life, the entities you want to be aligned with, where you want to focus your energy.

May you meet the upheaval of death in the place that keeps you surrounded by people and practices that serve your greater good.

when joy meets grief

What an unimaginable concept, right? *Joy meeting grief.* I recall thinking the same.

There is a momentous day after a death or loss, in the throes of grief, that most people will eventually experience. It might be three days, three weeks, three months, or it might be three years down the line.

For most people there comes a day when you catch yourself freely giggling or maybe even laughing hysterically or experiencing a quiet delight about the beauty of nature around you. Or maybe you are exercising, and a feeling of euphoria that had long taken leave washes over you. Or maybe you feel an excitement about your art or a creative process that grief had put on the back burner.

A time comes where you take notice, because it feels so different than what death had laid down before you.

What's this?

It's me, joy answers. *I'm still here.*

For a moment you may feel a twinge of guilt, because this feeling is so far removed from the grief you've been carrying. But if you are very observant, you may pause and say: *Wait, I get this*. It doesn't have to be either/or. It's actually possible to feel great joy *and* great grief at the same time. And at that point you may hear that bell ring again, marking the fact that you are at the fork in the road that calls you to *full-spectrum living*. Consider moving forward in that direction.

Feeling such expansion and giving yourself permission to hang out in that lighter place, for a while, does not signal moving on, nor leaving your loved one behind. There is no need to resist it.

This collision with happiness signals that you are opening to remembering love. Remembering joy. Remembering that you have choices to make, and your grief is saying: *It's okay, I'm ready to start riding in the back seat of the vehicle now—or at least sometimes.*

And above all, if you do experience twinges of guilt and maybe even a slight panic at the thought of *moving on,* as if finding peace or happiness again will somehow move you further from your person.

Pause.

Imagine your loved one in your mind's eye. Shut your eyes and breathe naturally, yet deeply and evenly. And from your heart, sit with the question: *Would my person have any resentment about me experiencing joy right now?*

Unequivocally, what we hear from people who have had near-death experiences, or have communicated with spirit in the afterlife, is that our loved ones' energy is able to experience their continuum in a much more light-filled and peaceful way when their survivors are able to move through their deep, deep anguish and allow themselves to reach out to joy.

I certainly have experienced the weight of feeling some survivor guilt—guilt that I'm still walking the planet and my loved ones aren't. Or a twinge of guilt when I began to experience joy.

There is no guarantee of a smooth ascent from the throes of grief. Rather, it may be the helicopter on a windy day that is attempting to lower the rescue basket and hoist you up. Joy may reel you up, but anger or heartbreak or frustration may cause the winds of change to blow, thrusting you about or lowering you again.

130

Be patient. Joy will whisper again.

The question is, will you be ready to answer?

May you consider answering when happiness and joy and lightheartedness calls you.

barely-there grief

Some people talk about having an experience within the aftermath of their loved one's death where extreme sadness did not remain or was barely noticed.

Maybe grief has had its way with you for a protracted time prior to your person's death and is moving through you and leaving you washed clean. Oh, that it could always stop in for that type of quick visit.

Maybe you are grounded in a belief system that sees death as a sweet release.

Or maybe you've shelved your grief. This is the version I want to caution you about. The thing is, thoughts and feelings surrounding your loved one's death will come out, one way or another, if they aren't adequately felt and processed. This may play out in your relationships, your functioning, your behaviors, but it will find a way out.

Be careful and do what you can to assure that it releases itself in a way that doesn't destroy other areas of your life and add to your turmoil. Anger, discord, overconsumption, overwork, oversleep, over-everything—all distractions from the fire that death left raging inside of you.

Not tending to the fire allows it to rage, uncontrolled and unrecognizable. And just when you think it may have been snuffed out, because you hope time will do that for you, a spark ignites another wildfire.

While there may always be a smoldering of deep grief within you, until you tend to your emotional terrain, the wildfires may continue to surprise and confuse you.

There are many, many stories of people decompensating after loss and experiencing destruction and deconstruction of their lives; in such cases, there are far more negative repercussions than walking through the valley of grief would have had.

If it's just too hard or you are feeling constricted and emotionally shut down, seek a professional to speak with who has experienced deep loss and personally understands the language of grief.

One way or another—*grief will have its way with you.*

Consider facing your grief, and calling it what it is, and tending to the beautiful-horrible left in its aftermath.

May you open to what grief asks of you, letting go of fear and keeping an eye on your evolution in this dance of life.

the reality of it all

One day, you will wake up, and instead of those blissful three seconds when you've forgotten your loved one has died, you will not have to remind yourself.

You will drive to work, or take your kids to school, or go for your morning walk, and no longer will you curse the fact that people are not recognizing that something life-altering has happened.

You'll nod at the people you pass. Maybe even smile or wave. And you will have hit an inner crossroads where you realize that you are not the only person that has gone through this deep suffering. That very person you've exchanged that knowing look with? Maybe their grief saw the grief in you.

You may very likely look at people differently forever more.

The person in the airport looking sullen, or sitting on the park bench with a hint of sadness in their expression, may tug at your heart. Now, because of the club you belong to, you may think, *I wonder if they are grieving right now.*

You may never fully come to terms with your loved one's absence from the planet, but you understand the reality of it. You are living it every day, and it is redefining how you walk in the world, how you talk in the world.

And that renewed compassion you have for others experiencing loss now lies deep within you, and it will forever be a spoke on your wheel of full-spectrum living, affecting the way you interact with the world around you.

The death of your loved one has transformed you. And transformation is an action that does not end until your own heart stops beating.

Allow their legacy to facilitate you being a kinder, more attentive, loving, compassionate person, and watch what blossoms from the gap where the love they left behind lives.

This is who you are now.

Today.

In this moment.

Different than you were before your great loss. And you will be different still tomorrow.

As every poignant moment of our life becomes embedded within our existence, so too will your great loss.

Whether you acknowledge and carry your loved one's passing with you, heart and eyes wide open, or it is buried in your layers of trying to let go—it is now forever tattooed on your heart.

This is your story now.

Love it as you loved your loved one.

Embrace it.

Honor it.

how long will grief live with you

The absence of your loved one will forever be a part of who you are now.

Give yourself some space and grace.

Try not to listen to the people giving you messages suggesting that you've grieved long enough. Try to remember that grief will have its unique way with you.

And that is normal. It's normal for grief to look different in every person. It is normal for grief to have no normal. It is okay to hurt and remember and love deeply, for as long as you need. It is normal to have periods where you think that maybe you have moved on and then to be slammed again by the depths of grief.

There is no right way.

There is only your way.

And speaking from experience, my friend, you can't decisively plan how grief will accompany you after deep loss.

Increasing your literacy and awareness about death and all the emotions it holds, you will be able to have a more pure and honest experience of grief. An experience not marred by clenching and hiding and fighting your emotions. An experience that recognizes that the intensity of your emotional response is directly related to the depth of the relationship and the love you had for the person who has died.

Jenifer shares three things she's learned about grief after the death of her husband, who ended his life:

- ○ It is not your fault.
- ○ Do not isolate. People want to help, so let them; even if it is to just sit with you.
- ○ Reach out for some kind of grief therapy as soon as possible. This could be a spiritual advisor as well. In the very early days, it is hard to make sense of anything and they can help you navigate.

Chrissie shares three things she learned about grief following the death of her partner, who ended his life:

- ○ Honor your feelings: The feelings of grief can range from despair and sadness, to anger and rage, all the way to numb. And you feel a bunch of contradicting feelings in a matter of minutes. It's all normal. Do not judge yourself, your feelings or how you grieve. It's hard enough to go through it without adding self-judgment on top of it..
- ○ Seek connection: Grief is a hell of a lonely journey. It's

possible that your closest family and friends may not be the ones to help you get through it. And that's okay. Find others who have gone through grief the way you have. And while grief is a personal journey, find those who understand to walk through it with you.

o   Don't compare your grief to others': There are no timelines or rules for grieving. I've fallen into this trap many times. I still do. But, you just have to honor your grief, yourself, and your loved one as makes sense for you. What works best for you is completely different than what works for others.

may grace befriend you as your grief moves through you

may you feel your love, feel their love, and know that love will bind you forevermore

may you understand that utter shock and disbelief is normal, and may you pause and remember love when those feelings of disbelief and anguish become overwhelming

break-ups: death can be the
great divide

i knew you once

then death knocked

you smelled the smoke

stopped-dropped-rolled

found the back door

crawled to safety

quietly

alone

forgetting to

call for a rescue

you left me

burning

H ave you ever felt abandoned in your loss?

If your answer is no, I'm so very happy for you.

Whenever we veer into conversations about people who've experienced friends jumping ship after great loss, it continues to blow me away how many hands slowly go up—*me too*.

Chances are you already have or will be touched by this phenomenon.

Hearing everyone's shock about some of their closest connections taking flight underlines the importance of acknowledging the unpleasant truth: it is possible that people you thought would be some of your most rock-solid supports soon perform a vanishing act.

First, let's look at our own history of handling this situation in the past. Can you recall a time when someone you knew, or were very close to, experienced a deep loss?

How have you shown up for others in their time of need?

This isn't meant to be provocative, but to give you pause to really sit with this question, because, in actuality, should we expect more from others than we are able to give ourselves? Acknowledging where we sit on that spectrum of giving compassion during others' difficult times is important. When we look honestly at how we've shown up for others around a time of death, we may find some answers about why we find people behaving in a hurtful manner. Chances are, it is all about their very own hurt—previous or anticipated.

If recollecting your previous actions finds you feeling *less-than*, you have permission to step out of the time-out chair. This introspection is not meant to point a finger at you personally.

We are a product of how the culture has treated death throughout time. If discourse, conversations, around death and dying were the norm, we would have had better lessons on how to do death, for ourselves and with others.

It's fair to unpack our own history of dealing with death and supporting others if we want to honestly look at how we are feeling when we've been abandoned during our time of grief.

Let us remember that we don't get to define *deep loss* for another human. That call rests solely in the heart of the griever. We need to make an effort to ignore the tendency to think things like: *For God's sake, it's just a dog, this has gone on too long.*

Modeling is the most powerful form of teaching, and if we were not exposed to role models doing death well—observing what support looks like after a death—we can find ourselves feeling as if we are barely keeping our head above water when attempting to sit with another's pain.

My personal experience and ability to show up for others has varied. At times I've truly been able to stay at a person's side, supporting, providing care, nourishment, and practical needs. But there have also been times when I haven't had the staying power.

Showing up for people outside my family was actually modeled for me throughout my childhood. What wasn't role-modeled was the emotional integrity needed to maintain that staying power over the long haul. I had to increase my awareness and stretch my muscles on that score.

Many of us have the capacity to show up whenever everyone else is—dropping off the food, offering our services, the *call if you need anything* offers.

What longevity of support for the grieving asks of us is to sign up for the long haul—continuing to check in and let the griever know we are there for them. Unequivocally, the *long haul* is where I've heard that people felt support was missing.

This can be tricky terrain, since we, as support people, don't always understand a person's baseline for processing death. If you've ever been met by a comment that *it hurts worse when you bring them up* or read about people who just want to be left alone and move on, it's enough to put a clamp on our good intentions, out of fear of doing more damage.

Sometimes we have heard repeatedly about how inept people's attempts at support have been.

While this may initially feel like the justified complaints of the griever who has been the recipient of some wonky condolences, based on the way people tick, continually complaining that it's never enough may have a paradoxical effect of scaring people away from supporting others.

How can they ever get it right? Why try?

And what may be the fatal error behind these complaints is something we easily forget: 100 percent of us will experience death and loss and grief. We are all wounded people, helping wounded people.

And those wounds and our experiences may actually have rendered us a bit broken when it comes to witnessing others' loss.

You see, this isn't an easy area to speculate or write about, because, as we know, every person's story is different. Every person is different. Every person's ability to communicate on an emotional level is different. Every person's ability to show up, to be present, is different.

The vast majority of humans in the throes of death and loss and grief unequivocally experience a sense of exhale when they feel seen and heard in a meaningful way.

How can someone be afraid to say their name? I'm thinking about them constantly. They aren't going to shock me.

This is a very common sentiment expressed by people who've had a loved one die.

Sometimes we forget the obvious when we are trying to provide support for the griever: Ask.

I want to be here for you when you need me. I want you to feel seen by me. Please tell me what that looks like for you. (listen)

Just let me know if I'm ever being too much and you need space—I would totally understand.

Can I take you for a drive and we can just be together? We don't need to talk if you don't want to.

How's your heart today?

Let them know they can change their minds about what support looks like, and you are open to listening.

We are rarely reminded of the twists and turns of grief and the varying emotions it can trigger: anger, frustration, loneliness, feeling misunderstood, one minute feeling like you've reached some sense of closure and the next the scab being ripped off, and once again you are raw and weeping.

Grief is not linear, and since we aren't taught about it, twisty, winding roads can scare people.

Especially those people who have been programmed to believe that Elisabeth Kübler-Ross' Five Stages are linear and the final authority on grief. Again, a reminder that she created those stages in reference to people who have just received a terminal diagnosis. Denial, anger, bargaining, depression, acceptance. The stages, and their order, make so much more sense in that context—and not so much sense when it's suggested that grief after a death proceeds predictably.

May we understand the power of benevolent presence as we travel with others during their grieving process and, when grieving, may we recognize the presence of others.

when awkwardness hits

Not only do you have to contend with your own big feelings at the time of loss, but there is still a whole wide world out there. In that world there may be close and distant family, friends, neighbors, colleagues, those you bump into occasionally—all sorts of social networks. And all of those interactions, especially immediately after your loss, have the potential to feel awkward.

There may be the friend who always greets you with a big "Heeeeyy, how are you doing?" And that might just slip out before they catch themselves, leaving you standing in shock, thinking: *What the actual fuck?*

Trust me, they will regret the fact they do not have a superpower of disappearing into thin air as soon as words like those came out of their mouth. None of us want to show up as an asshole to others when great loss strikes.

Unless you are gifted with empathy, and experienced with giving comfort, there will be times you will find yourself at a loss for words in the aftermath of death. And even the person who is smooth with their condolences can sometimes be crucified for being so polished, they can't possibly be genuine.

If you've perused the death and dying areas online and in social media, you've seen the insults slung about how people show up and the words they share after a death.

There are all sorts of condolence phrases, and almost all can garner criticism. Even the well-thought-out ones that we use when we pick our brains to be genuine.

"I'm sorry for your loss." *What are they sorry for; they didn't do anything. Loss? I haven't lost something. My person is dead.*

"Everything happens for a reason." *What the actual fuck? My person wasn't meant to die. Don't tell me there was a reason.*

"They are in a better place." *Bullshit. How can they even suggest that being with me isn't the better place.*

"I'm holding you in my heart." *What does that actually mean. I'm standing right here. And how does that help me?*

As we discussed earlier, we are all the walking wounded. Your loss may be triggering someone else's painful experience and affecting their ability to state the words that would better support your specific situation. The walking wounded may be sharing words with you that brought them great comfort, but the same words just don't resonate for you.

Please understand that by shutting down these conversations

143

and attempts at providing support, we are pushing conversations surrounding death and dying further into the closet.

Who will be brave enough to venture into the land of condolences if they are seeing gangs of people shaming others for not doing it *right?*

The answer is: *eventually, no one.*

We've observed an undercurrent of grievers fueled with negative energy towards those who show up awkwardly. I'm simply trying to point out the fact that it may be helpful to acknowledge that they *are* making an attempt at showing up.

Attacking the awkward condolence giver can be an addictive form of displacement, where the flammable ether of your grief sparks indignant anger.

Just be aware.

Be careful you are speaking your own truth and not jumping on someone else's train of shaming others, because the cold, hard fact is that when someone is experiencing deep or tragic loss, it's impossible to land on perfect words of comfort.

There are no words.

Death, dying and the aftermath are challenging enough to walk towards, but if we have to walk on eggshells and worry that we are going to be shamed for our words, it may create a wave of people simply too scared to show up.

Most grievers don't initially have the energy to take advantage of teachable moments, in the manner of: *Actually, that phrase doesn't comfort me; if you would be so kind to just say … that makes more sense for me.*

By all means, you can consider circling around and having the conversation with someone at some point when you are able. Or you may consider simply accepting that they were likely doing their best in that moment.

Admittedly, there are some responses that are unacceptable. A person who has experienced a death of someone should never be told they are grieving wrong or inappropriately.

When people are sending messages such as: *Shouldn't you be over*

144

this by now? they are really adding two silent words: *for me*. Between the lines rests the sentiment: *This is so hard, watching you suffer for so long; I wish you could feel better and we could get back to normal.*

One consideration highlighted by this trend of people complaining about awkward condolences is the fact that many of us are on one *spectrum* or another.

Only in the last couple of decades have we recognized that some people have ways of being that make connecting socially and empathically a challenge. That means we have a world of people walking the earth who always struggle socially. Is it possible that some of the people who show up awkwardly are part of that struggle as well? Just something to consider if we're attempting to live in a way that puts an empathic foot forward.

The path to showing up for others, after death, is sharp and twisted; it's a place of uncertainty. It can be a beautiful thing, seeing people attempt to give heartfelt condolences— maybe we can also feel the effort in their *try*, even when it's clunky.

If you have one person who is by your side for the deep and treacherous terrain of your life— the person who can sit with your hard stories and emotional implosions— you are a lucky person.

If not, try to find that person in a therapist or spiritual advisor and lay down your burden with them, expecting to be met with genuine compassion.

We are in a very egocentric space when death visits; our feelings are, of course, all about us and our relationship to the deceased.

We are likely to be emotionally and physically exhausted, and it makes sense that this is a time when we are not spontaneously considering the feelings of others. You are not meant to over-care for others when your grief is so acute.

The bottom line is that death and grief can suck and feel raw, and sometimes there really are no adequate words.

If you find yourself really wanting to bang on about the ineptitude of others during your time of loss, let's look the elephant in the room straight in its big, beautiful, tear-swollen eyes.

Distraction and *projection* are very real coping mechanisms subconsciously employed to help us through difficult times. There are times we spend excessive energy distracting ourselves from what is really hurting us by projecting our pain onto something else.

DON'T LOOK AWAY

shared by Margo Fowkes
whose son, Jimmy, died of cancer
Founder of Salt Water
Find Your Harbor

When someone dear to us dies, we need our friends and family to lean in, to show up, to offer words of love and comfort.

Google "how to help a friend who is grieving" and article after article will appear about what not to say, written in a tone that implies there are words that will repair the grief, make it better, heal the other person's pain. Instead of being helpful, these articles often feed people's natural fear about saying or doing the wrong thing, resulting in them pulling away, avoiding their grieving loved one, saying nothing at all.

When friends called to check on me after my son Jimmy died of brain cancer, I discovered I didn't care how they phrased their concern. Most of the time, I was too numb to hear the exact words anyway, but I didn't miss the love behind them. On any given day, I might be too shattered to say how I was, but it was never lost on me that they cared enough to ask.

We don't always say or do the "right" thing when we reach out to a grieving loved one. Death is shattering and grief is scary. If you haven't lost one of your essential people, how could you possibly know what to say or how to help someone who has?

Sometimes I think we make this grief stuff too compli-

146

cated. We want so badly to stop feeling broken that we buy into the notion that our friends and family can and should fix our pain.

Contrary to what grievers are led to believe, perfect phrases and magic words don't exist. No one can bring my son back or repair the Jimmy-size hole in my heart. What does help is showing up, sitting with me while I cry, sharing memories and stories about Jimmy, saying what's true—that you don't know what to say; that you miss him, too; that you're here and you promise not to look away.

the inept

Yes, I heard your internal whispers while reading the above section.

And yes, you are right, there are some people who are just going to be inept. Mean, even. Some people have personality issues that make the aftermath of death a playground that can make our sorrow feel even more torturous.

Those are not your people.

Some individuals won't show up in a compassionate way that honors the sacredness needed to meet the survivors of someone who died; we have all heard (or experienced) the stories. That, my friend, is when you call on your lessons on personal boundaries and you firmly set them in stone.

Boundaries, you say?

The only boundary I know about it is the fence we put up to keep our neighbors from peeking in.

Yes, *that* friend.

That, except it's your tender heart and soul that need the protection. Explore information that gives you permission to set boundaries in your life and then call on those lessons when death knocks on the door.

Oh I can't have boundaries with people I love, it isn't kind.

147

Actually, it is unkind to *not* have interpersonal boundaries. Your emotional enmeshment with others can be holding them back from doing the work they need to do to be their best selves. An important concept to keep in mind is called *detachment with love*.

Sometimes it is a hard and painful act of love to back out of someone's life and set some perimeters around where you will meet each other, but that detachment can free their bound roots and give them space to grow with abandon in the direction universal energy is asking them to expand.

Yes, maybe that growth will not happen, but that is their choice, not ours.

And, yes, it quite possibly may look hard and shitty for a while, but hold back and let them do their work.

In alignment with this concept, if unhelpful or hurtful people show up during your time of bereavement, you have permission to ask them to give you space so you can work on your own healing. Anyone who can't respect such a request requires even more firm boundaries.

Maybe we would all be better served by taking an occasional personal inventory:

Who is in my life that has capacity to sit with me and my big emotions?
Who is able to provide support and help without being obtrusive?
Whose presence feels like it is more helpful than hurtful?

A further consideration as we look at our own *advanced planning* is giving some thought to who you may want in your intimate circle during life's most difficult times.

control

One of the most complicated aspects after a death is to experience someone abandoning you. I'd like to say this doesn't frequently happen, but I'd be lying.

Why is this a thing?

Lack of control is one reason. There is nothing as much out of our power as death, and when it strikes, whether expected or unexpected, people we'd least expect it from can manifest surprising behavior.

148

Rather than dealing with the big emotions, sometimes people previously close to us choose to pick away at minutia until it creates an enormous chasm: how post-death plans are handled, wills and division of property, the way you grieve, the way you didn't grieve ... and these altercations can turn into lifelong rifts.

Sometimes the people you thought were your rocks are unable to fully show up because of their own issues. They may hurl conflict like they're at a shooting range, sending the clay targets of pain flying overhead, daring you to fire a shot.

Another consideration is that we can be both a griever and a person who hasn't given adequate support to others who are grieving.

How? you might ask. *How can that happen?*

Because we are human, and death, loss, grief, and trauma bring out big feelings and underlying issues, and it is an ever-changing terrain. When our pain is so immense we may be in such an egocentric space that we are not inclined to take others' hurting into consideration; grief's vision can be myopic.

After experiencing great loss, people sometimes can't handle how you now show up in the world. And guess what? If that is the case, *those are not your people.*

Yes, they may stay in the background and, after *a cooling down period,* slowly tiptoe around the corner and catch your eye. Then, only you can decide if you are able to welcome them back into your lives. Those folks cannot control how your emotions may show up and, unknowingly, poke at their own vulnerability; they may find it too challenging to remain with you for the long term.

The thing is—that ache from your loved one not being on the planet any longer will never totally leave you. You may find that the criteria for your nearest and dearest to remain close to you is their staying power when you are struggling with big feelings.

You've learned the lesson: there are no guarantees you won't experience this type of pain again, and for people who must feel in constant control, that may send them running.

Remember, you get to write the rules of how you walk in this world and who you want by your side. Choose wisely, and dig deeper into the concept of interpersonal boundaries if you need space to keep yourself safe.

death changes you

I had a long career working with people, with the advantage of an advanced degree and experience in therapeutic intervention.

My father died when I was 22. A complex relationship yielded a complex grief process.

I thought *I got it.*

Then after my brother, and nine months later my mother, who lived with us, died, I *got it* on an entirely new level. Their deaths were my initiation into losing a piece of my best self, my lifelong soul-connects. My longest supports.

Their deaths shook me on a cellular level. My brain was broken by their absence in my life. I am not the same person.

Understand that your *friends* may not recognize you anymore. Your pain and loss may scare them for a variety of reasons: you've blown their ability to stay in denial about death; they've never learned how to sit with someone who is hurting; they are so wrapped up in their own lives, they don't have time to be with friends during *the hard*. (The age-old term *fair weather friends* comes to mind.)

There's an infinite number of reasons people you thought had your back disappear.

Remember this. It is not about *you*. Not personally.

It is about *them*. Personally. They aren't equipped to handle what you now bring to the table.

You may allow these people to circle back into your life somewhere down the line, but ultimately? Take tender care of yourself in making that decision.

You are not alone. So many people have had the experience of being abandoned. I've heard story after story and, like I said, I've experienced this as well. Personally, the couple of folks who have retreated from our lives have caused me to address an important life lesson.

I typically have put myself in the position of being the connector, and for the past ten years I've really been working at not putting more energy into relationships or resolving conflict than the other people do. It's about self-respect and not being so desperate for connection that you accept malicious, dishonest, or less than authentic relationships.

Having practiced that a bit as I've aged, it has become more clear to me that it is not my duty to chase people down to try to fix whatever they perceive as broken—the reason they had to exit.

At this point in my life, if people aren't able to meet me with honesty and a desire to continue the relationship, I am mindful not to swoop in to make it all better.

A helpful rule is to not work harder on someone else's issues than they are willing to.

The sad part is that people are so death-averse, and therefore behave in such wonky ways to avoid its discomfort, that their issues with death may well herald the death of relationships.

If you are feeling lonely or abandoned after death has visited, try connecting with someone who has had similar experiences.

But most of all?

Connect deeply with yourself.

Honor your path.

Honor your loved one.

Honor the fact that life may feel different now.

Stay in touch with and honor your beautiful-horrible truth.

couples: judging each other's grieving

This is a sad conversation.

Various numbers are thrown around, but the first statistic that came up in my search? Eighty percent of marriages end after the loss of a child.

I recently read that the primary reason for this phenomenon is judging each other's manner of grieving.

Thanks to a groundbreaking book called *The Five Love Languages* that, back in the day, landed in the hands of every couples' counselor *and* many couples, we've become more adept at understanding that individuals express and perceive love in their own unique ways.

The same awareness is important around grief. We all have our own individual grief languages.

We may think we know what the other person is thinking, or feeling, just by observing them. Unfortunately, that's not the case.

Some people retreat in their relationships. On the other extreme, some openly express big, strong emotions each and every day. And there are myriad expressions of grief in between.

If people differ in their capacity for *the hard*, and in their ways of managing it, that can mark the breaking point in a relationship.

Don't you even care? You never talk about them anymore.

It's all you talk about, I can't do it anymore, I have to have a break, it's destroying me.

And everything in between.

Unfortunately, most of the time those sentences aren't said out loud, but live in our vault of silent judgments, silently multiplying.

If we could have these difficult conversations and get to the place where we understand each other's grieving style and needs surrounding loss, maybe the distance between partners wouldn't keep growing.

Some of the most successful partnerships I've spoken with, post-death, have enlisted some professional help proactively because they are cognizant of the statistics and do not want to become one of them.

Let me also share that sometimes it's just about staying-power. The terrain after the death of a loved one will inevitability hold times where partners' emotions feel incompatible.

Unpredictability, volatility, triggers, ups, downs, silence, retreating. The list goes on.

My husband and I met while working as helpers. He was a cardiologist with a holistic view, and I was on his team as the mind–body therapist.

One of the most endearing things about him was watching him with people who were dying. One day, fairly early in our relationship, he was late coming home for the meal I had prepared for our brood. It was because he'd sat by a dying patient's bedside and read them their beloved poetry.

Yes, he had my heart at the bedside of death.

Flash-forward fifteen years, when we have our own dates with the deaths of primary loves. First my brother's untimely death from brain cancer. Nine months later, my mother's narrated and openly processed death while living with us. Two months later, my husband's father's sudden death. Six months later, his mother, and more recently another brother. Wedged in there was the unexpected death of a beloved pup, which the pet-lovers here will understand fully added insult to our heartbreaking injury. All of these deaths and aftermaths had their own brand of complications. Death is rarely simple.

My complicated childhood and relationships brought complex grief experiences.

In contrast, he had a pretty straightforward upbringing, under the British flag of *stiff upper lip* and the *be strong* messages of the *just get on with it* variety. Thankfully he wasn't the town crier of that message during our time of grieving. He understood the contrast in our experiences. There was a fairly wide chasm between our differing methods of grieving.

My ever-empathic doctor husband actually wasn't so much the emoter with our own loss. He went quiet. A little edgy at times. Distanced. Subtly controlling with nurturing behavior—I know that sounds like an oxymoron, but it's the plight of someone whose love-language is *acts of service*.

He threw himself into being the gentleman farmer, planting an orchard. And yes, there were times when we met in the middle, but he couldn't stay in the space of my *raw* for too long at a time.

Myself?

I couldn't hide my devastation and did my own bit of retreating, but also formed a little thing called *The Death Dialogues Project* and conducted interviews with *my people* (the openly grieving, the processsors), staged productions and workshops, started a podcast, made connections online … all things that he has been extremely supportive of.

In between bursts of activity I might take to the bed, as I have a serious autoimmune condition, easily exacerbated by stress; fatigue is one of its most annoying symptoms.

My husband and I were very aware that this was the place where a relationship can skid off the road, but the magic for us was simply acknowledging that fact and putting something into place—wait for it; it's such a clinical term—*staying power.*

Staying power that consisted of: *You are my person. Period.*

You can ugly-cry, yell in frustration, need your space, take to the bed, withdraw, but I get this is how grief is having its way with you, and I will be here.

Did we say those words? Not always.

The reality of what we were doing wasn't acknowledged until a good friend departed our orbit, and that action shone a light on the fact that love during deep grief, for us, looks like *not* retreating.

Simply showing up.

Every damned day.

We can't be everything for each other.

Ultimately it is my responsibility to be there for myself and take care of my emotional needs, even if that means getting assistance from an outside source. And, however we are both doing, whether it's going quiet and planting an orchard, or reaching out into the world to speak of our loss, we shall be there for each other on the other side.

We are each other's ride and die; death has taught us that much is true.

May you look through your lens of patience at those who are there for you.

your people: finding a sense of home

In the aftermath of everything we've talked about here, you may find yourself lonely and not knowing where to turn.

Many of the people I have met faced this issue.

Even those close to them would give them messages implying they weren't grieving fast enough.

Repeatedly, people have hopped off Facebook and onto Instagram, which most grievers find kinder and gentler. To avoid being found by those who have disapproved of their grief process, many do not initially have their name with their account, so they can share freely and soak in the anonymity of it all. And the connections. The people who say to them, *I get it.*

And then something happens.

Others who resonate with their messages reach out. Suddenly the person isn't feeling so alone anymore. They feel heard. Seen. Understood.

And many times, finding this level of experiencing and talking about all of their big feelings, something is born of the loss and grief.

Maybe it's a movement or community for other people who can relate. Maybe it's a mission or practice.

There's such beauty seeing some of these people decide to physically meet up with others—IRL is how the kids say it: *in real life*—they have met from around the world, finding a bond forged by death.

Where can *you* find people who *get it?*

Are there local grief groups you could attend? My sister-in-law still regularly attends hers and feels a deep sense of connection from the experience.

Your church or other social community?

How about that one person who had a similar loss and you didn't know them that well, or maybe didn't show up for in the way you now wish you would have?

Chances are *they* will get you. You could consider asking them to meet you for a cuppa.

It may not feel like a simple task, finding a support network. And

155

many of us find our mattress and pillow to be just the support we need for a good long while, *thank-you-very-much*. But quite possibly a day will come when you want more.

You're tired of going to work or marching through your daily structure and obligations in a robotic fashion because you dare not say anything that might make people nervous. Your gaze begins to search for others who may get it.

When that time comes, don't forget that there are villages of those people who have walked similar walks all over the world, and they are just waiting for you to come home.

"Before our son died we were part of a very large and close-knit group of friends. My two closest friends before he died became my two furthest friends afterwards, going two completely separate direc-tions with what may have been their grief. The first friend became attention-seeking. Since I withdrew socially, she became a self-proclaimed spokesperson, talking about me to large groups of people, using my situation to elevate herself above others to discuss private details, her opinions, and to tell people how to treat me appropriately during this time. This behavior drew me far away. The second friend's behavior was almost exactly the opposite. She grew so tired (and jealous) of the attention I was receiving that she tried to convince people not to hang out with our family anymore. She would tell people about how much we've changed for the worse, and would plan things excluding us, encouraging others to do the same. This drew others away from us. We could no longer carry on any superficial relationships after this tragedy. Sadly, I didn't even realize that all of these friendships were superficial until this became our reality. Our current close friends either have gotten to know us since our son's passing or are friends who didn't know him well because our relationships never revolved around our children."

– anonymous

may you always remember to show up for yourself

may you understand more deeply who is in your life who has the capacity to stay

may we stay present and hold the truth that death is an inevitability of life—
living and loving with abandon

love never dies—
do not ignore signs

when soft like time

came through the mist

the outline of your face

i felt the gentle of your nudge

a whisper—this is grace

As I continued to hear people's stories surrounding death, I soon discovered that our experiences of dying and death aren't the only secrets we keep. This section explains most of what I mean when I speak of death, dying and *the aftermath*.

Most assume I'm only speaking about our emotional aftermath, when in fact, I'm also referring to the *what's next* regarding your connection with your loved one after they die.

The vast majority of people have had an experience where they feel they have sensed a connection with a deceased loved one.

Even though my mother was very religious (Christian), we would have conversations about the spirit world, beginning when I was a child and even more as adults; especially so in her last two years of life, when she lived with us. Therefore, a part of me was always open and intrigued about these stories. From the onset of the project, I started making a habit of asking people during interviews: *Have you had an experience where you think you've been in contact with your deceased loved one?*

Honestly, hearing the answers to that question is one of the personal rewards of gathering stories.

Almost everyone has shared accounts of feeling connection with their deceased person. Commonly in literature and reports, there appear to be more stories of this phenomenon occurring relatively soon after death, but we also hear of experiences decades later.

161

On the morning of September 11, 1983, at 5 a.m., suddenly awakened after the first night my mother, my brother, and I spent at our family home after my father died, we had an undeniable experience of my father's spirit communicating.

You can listen to *The Death Dialogues Project Podcast* Episode 8, "Ghost stories: love never dies" to hear that story in its entirety.

When we arrived back to my parents' home, I went into my father's bedroom and saw his clothes hanging on the hook in his closet, just where he'd mindfully hung them, clearly waiting for him to step into them the next day.

I felt the rattling coins and keys in his pocket that had always clink-clanked his arrival as he walked up our steps, cuing me to do any last-minute clearing and quickly hide away.

In that moment, I was overcome with a visceral sense of *knowing*, deep in my bones, that our energy, soul, essence—whatever you may call it—does not die or end when our physical body takes leave.

And then, in the morning, at the dawn-crack hour of his usual awakening, my father's spirit-energy proved that point beyond a reasonable doubt.

Later, I was running an Adult Partial Hospitalization Program that focused on helping people with mood and anxiety issues, sometimes with co-occurring substance/alcohol abuse and/or eating disorders. The daughter of the nurse in the program had experienced the sudden death of a young friend and introduced me to the book *Hello from Heaven,* by researcher team Bill and Judy Guggenheim. They had been asked by Elisabeth Kübler-Ross to put out a call to people who felt they'd had contact with a loved one after their death.

Expecting minimal response, they were flooded with stories. This lovely book is broken into chapters of common experiences of after-death communication (ADC). It's a fascinating read, empowering us to start noticing those moments of coincidence and synchronicity a bit more after a loved one's passing.

My brother died in January 2017; my mother in October of that year. With each of them, pacts were made that whoever died first would give the other signs—and they have.

After the first sign, I started keeping a running list on my mobile phone's notes section so I wouldn't forget. As time has passed, I don't always write them down, but it's a great source of connection when I do read them.

Through this practice of understanding the possibility of ADC, my grief burden has been lightened. The love and history and connection with both of them is deep, and it's beautiful to have, but that doesn't negate the fact that there are still times the lack of their physical presence is excruciating.

I've heard a renowned medium say after the loss of one of their loved ones: *Even with my connection to the beyond, I still miss my loved one being on the planet. That's part of being human.* The gift of connection did not make them immune to deep grief.

Staying open to my people's ongoing love-energy, and exploring the topic, and hearing experiences shared for the project, my full-spectrum experience of living has deepened and widened. The relationship with my deceased loved ones continues as we exchange love-energy.

I consider my mom and brother to be part of my *team* on the other side.

Brought up in a home with fundamentalist Christian doctrine, even as a young child, my inner knowing was that the absolutes about life, death and the afterlife seemed fear-based and were used as a threat to keep people compliant.

Personally, I worship at the feet of the great mystery, believing in *all love* in the afterlife. This leaves me in awe of what the journey may eventually look like for myself.

From my interviews and exploration, including stories of near-death experiences, which give us a fascinating perspective, it appears that you are met by whatever and whomever your belief system holds. If you believe your mother and brother will be there to greet you when you *cross over*, as my mother called it as she was transitioning, they will be waiting for you.

My mother expected to be greeted by her people and in the last six hours was occasionally calling out "Mama." After the first time she called out, I asked her if her mother was there to help with her transition, and she nodded yes.

As my mother breathed her last breath, her gorgeous face brightened and a wash of knowing came over her, and her broad, beaming, yet relaxed smile told me that *yes, she was being greeted by her loves.* Mind you, this peaceful presence was a stark contrast to her facial expression, even a moment before, when she appeared already *gone.* Even my husband, who is not as embedded in these areas of exploration, excitedly leaned in and said: "Well done, go give [my deceased brother] a big hug for us."

Interestingly, her face filled with a radiant coloring that lasted until she left our home. No death pallor. There was much more palpable magic within her dying process.

Those moments were such a gift of affirmation for us. Much like our experience after our father died, and the lengthy list of happenings I've kept since.

Barbara Karnes, RN, an early icon from the hospice movement, affirmed that you won't find a nurse within a hospice who doesn't have stories of deceased loved ones escorting patients to the other side.

Reporting in from the field of near-death experiences, we hear the connection between one's beliefs or degree of openness and the experience of the dying: people who believe there is nothing more than darkness after death will likely experience just that. People who are counting on a reckoning at the pearly gates will experience something similar to that. People have seen their deceased baby or child being held by Jesus or Mother Mary; those people's belief systems were grounded in such tenets.

I reckon my mama may have seen her Jesus, too, along with her beloveds, whom she expected to accompany her to the other side.

We can expand so greatly if we try not to exhibit too much control, and frankly, concern about what the afterlife may or may not be. The overriding message from people who have experienced near-death is that it is all about *love*.

Some examples of connection we've heard through the project::

o Visitation in dreams: on awakening having a very deeply visceral response of *that was real*
o Seeing items or images of something that resonates with the loved one: hearts, coins, feathers, rainbows, so on, with these signs connected to a deep sense of knowing
o Electrical shenanigans where none previously existed, during a time that would seem relevant for connection
o Spontaneous thoughts that feel like communication
o Visualizing or hearing their loved one

During our first *Death Dialogues Project* production, the lights were blinking during sharing about a passed loved one. This hadn't happened previously and didn't happen after. Someone later said: *I noticed [my brother] showed up.*

Maybe it was my brother. But I suspect it was Mahyan, the little boy we were presenting that night, who had died years earlier. Maybe he showed up because there was so much loving energy in the room showing up for him.

And maybe it all boils down to what Einstein said: "Energy cannot be created or destroyed; it can only be changed from one form to another." And it's ours to stay open to how that energy shows up in our lives.

I sat on the jury at a murder trial, and just at the time of particularly descriptive information about the woman's death being shared for the first time, the power was lost in the courtroom. Darkness. The courtroom was full of her loved ones and the accused was her partner. We had to adjourn. People have experienced similar happenings surrounding funerals.

Many people report having seen an image of a loved one: I've heard a variety of stories along those lines.

One person I spoke with had a son who had died suddenly. She heard her daughter crying from the living room; she walked in, and she could see him from behind as he sat next to his sister, his hoodie pulled up over his head. Her mother's instinct felt he was comforting his sister. As if he sensed the mother's presence, she observed him rise and walk down the hall. When she went to the couch, there was an imprint where he had been sitting. Her daughter was unaware of his presence.

People report something I've seen referred to as "drop-in" visitations, where they see their person within the environment. I experienced this after my father died, while driving to visit my mother. I saw my father at the wheel of an oncoming car as it drove by. He smiled and nodded. And yes, it freaked me out, but there was also a *knowing*. I knew my father was dead *and* I knew the person looked exactly like him. I assumed it was a hello. I wouldn't hear about the concept of *drop-in visitations* for many years, and when I did, I was immediately reminded of this memory.

Interestingly, even though my father was a very difficult person to live with, he became an expert at connecting from the beyond, and I have frequently wondered if that, in part, is his way of attempting to make amends.

I came to believe the possibility that my father, whose anguished soul had such difficulty connecting with pure love energy and expressing love while alive, deeply wanted to communicate in that vibration he was able to tap into on the other side.

Drop-in visitations are ripe for responses of: *Aw, her grief is so severe her mind is playing tricks on her.*

If you are reading this and you've had an experience where you felt, *hmm, could this be a sign,* and then you let go of it, I'd like to encourage you to consider the possibility that, *yes, it could have been contact.*

And if you are reading this and desire this type of connection, try to regularly make some pleasant, quiet space for yourself and just breathe evenly while putting the request out to your loved ones. I've seen this type of grounding practice recommended from a variety of resources. The earlier mentioned breath-work is perfect as a foundation for that type of calming and centering practice.

Personally, I regularly have conversations with my loves when I'm alone in nature. And not only do I talk, I tune into any feelings or *messages* I feel I'm receiving; it can become a two-way conversation of sorts.

Notice the thoughts that randomly pop into your head that sound like your loved one. My research has regularly described communication between the living and dead as *telepathic*.

One suggestion from the pages of *Hello from Heaven* is to consider all those times you've heard or seen or smelled or experienced something that, for a moment, you considered to be connection, then said to yourself: *Nah, it had to be a coincidence.* Consider those times and then remind yourself, maybe it wasn't coincidence at all, but connection, and attempt to take more notice of those little taps on the shoulder.

Here is one of my stories of connection that was so powerful, even you can experience it with me:

My mother and I were always open surrounding the topics of death, dying and spirit connection, and she spoke frequently of her death even before living with me for the final two years of her life, when she was well into her nineties.

Celebrating her 93rd birthday a month after moving in with us, there was no denying what stage of life she was in, and that was not lost on her, as notices of the death of friends younger than herself arrived regularly.

Ever since my father died in 1983, we'd promised each other that whoever died first would give signs to the other.

Fast-forward to the 24 hours between my mom announcing, "I'm going to die now" and her last breath. She narrated her dying process as long as she had energy to do so, and at one point, with her energy waning, I said, "Everything I read talks about having the choice to exist at the age that you prefer, and it seems like people choose the time in their lives they felt most alive. What do you think that age would be for you?"

She let out a deep, exhausted sigh and moaned, "Oh, I don't know, this age, I guess."

I was quite aware that, based on some earlier comments about how her life had dragged on and on, and what she had previously shared about her happiest times in life, this answer didn't resonate. I actually felt guilty for asking anything of her when she was so clearly exhausted. Dying can be hard work. I couldn't resist, however, sliding in the reminder about connecting with me from the beyond, to which she exhaled, "If I can figure out how."

After she died, a death that beheld its own proof of her arrival in the afterlife, I was keeping my list of wee signs from my mama when a couple of friends came over for a walk in the hilly New Zealand countryside behind our home. Later I received a photo from one of them with the instruction: please look at this and let me know if you see anything.

Immediately, I saw an image of my mother's angled profile from the rear right of her.

It was distinctly her, from a time when my mother had many photographs taken of her, showing her being young and silly and fun-loving. In fact, this short window was probably the happiest and most carefree of her entire life. Newly moved out of the family home, where she'd experienced a poverty-ridden Oklahoma dustbowl upbringing, during the Great Depression. A daughter of sharecroppers, she'd picked cotton until her fingers bled when she was three years old. And in this window, she had yet to meet my father. The image of my mother was from that more carefree time.

Undeniably, I have received that sign as my mother's message as: *Here, this is the age I've landed on.* And yes, I guess I have figured this communication thing out.

Everyone who has seen this photo has seen the image in the sky with no coaxing. What stood out to me was her unmistakable profile and her big, gorgeous hair, which had been longer, as it appears in the clouds, during those younger years. The precise linear nature of the profile is so staggering that I no longer see a cloud in that portion of the photo.

Tina Marie Fluharty generously shares with us how her knowing about connection into the beyond arrived:

Before telling my story, you need to know a little about my Rebecca.

She was a force of nature—an old soul with a wild and creative spirit. She had the ability to find beauty in decay in her photography. She wasn't just beautiful—she had a laugh that was from her gut. She was tattooed, pierced, had a smile that would stop traffic, could curse like a sailor—but believed in God. Her favorite places to photograph were abandoned churches—all over the world.

June 2, 2018, was like any other day. Our family had a wedding coming up and Becca was to be the photographer for all of the events leading up to her cousin's big day. On June 2 we (all the girls) were getting together to have a contest to see who could create the flower arrangements for the wedding— using silk flowers and collected vases, we were each going to make an arrangement; then we would vote, and the winning arrangement would be taken to the florist to recreate in real flowers. It was mostly an excuse to drink a lot of wine and spend the weekend together. Becca was driving down from Philly for the event—our last communication was about a photo that she had sent me that arrived dented. My last text to her was, "I love everything you do." Her last text to me was a big red heart and, "I'll call you in a bit."

I was getting concerned because 5:00 was rolling around and she wasn't there yet. At exactly 4:30 p.m. (this time is important), I can only describe what happened as a rip in reality occurred—it was as if every cell, idea, known fact in the universe shifted for me. That last sentence doesn't even come close to describing what I experienced—it wasn't of this world. My family saw it happen—my sis in law saw my face turn white and my hands start shaking. I immediately said that something awful had happened and we needed to find Becca. I immediately called my son at Cherry Point (he is a Harrier pilot in the Marines) and told him to find his sister—screaming at him. I called her phone several times only to get voice mail. I even posted on her boyfriend's Facebook, "Where is Rebecca?" (I had never posted anything to him ever before.) My family was watching this happen with confusion—agreeing that something was wrong but trying to convince me that she was okay at the same time. My last text before leaving the house, "Becca, I am sending someone to find you if you don't call me back." I left the house for the drive from the Eastern Shore to my home in Annapolis.

About halfway, I stopped on the side of the road and called the police in south Philly—asking them to do a wellness check on her apartment (something I have never done for anyone). I called her dad in Florida and told him to get on his way up here to MD —he thought I was nuts but said he was on his way.

The drive home was in blinding rain (the kind where you need to pull over and wait it out)—and here is where my experience took a different turn. I was literally talking out loud, begging the universe to make what I already knew to be a lie. All of a sudden I was absolutely, without doubt, aware of another presence in my car—sometimes sitting next to me, sometimes just outside of the car. Again, no good words to describe it—it was very strong and very comforting—I felt it guiding me through the storm to get home. I never actually saw a form, but there was something there! It was there!

When I got home about an hour later, my phone rang as I walked into the house at about 7:30—it was a detective from

170

another part of Philly asking if I was Rebecca's mom, he was asking about her purse, and didn't seem to know about my wellness check call at first. It took several frantic minutes for everyone to put together that they were searching for "the woman swept away by flood waters" in the northern part of Philly—the same woman that a mother called a wellness check for in south Philly an hour prior. The search quickly turned into a recovery—I won't go into all the details—but my Becca was gone, having hit her head and drowned. Her boyfriend was also swept away but made it out—otherwise we would never have known what happened. I learned later that at exactly 4:30 he saw her go under in the raging flood and she stopped communicating with him. He said he knows it was exactly 4:30 because his phone was in his hand and under the water, but he could still see it lit up and it said 4:30. He said he thought it was weird that it was still working as he did not have a waterproof phone. He did not know about my experience until a day later when we went to him in the hospital.

If you have read this far (thank you if you have), my take-away is this. I am 1000% positive that what I felt at 4:30 was my Becca reaching out to me—what I interpreted as terrifying and horrible in the moment has turned into a source of comfort and hope. If my girl can find me at the moment of her transition and I can feel it—that is proof to me that we are all connected, both in this life and in the next, and in between also. If we are all energy (which we are), and the law of conservation of energy applies, then what and who we are never dies—and our connection to one another never dies either. It just takes on a different form—a beautiful, all-knowing form. I feel like I was given a tiny, tiny glimpse of that when she moved on—have found such peace in knowing that—and it feels like an absolute "knowing." And the "person" who rode with me home, while I was processing what I already knew was there, to also comfort and guide me home—it was

171

such a strong force, and it was real.

I was raised as a Methodist, spent some time in the Assembly of God churches, but do not attend church anymore—but I kept my "faith." But I feel I learned more on the day my girl passed on than I ever did in any church pew or Sunday school. I feel I was given proof that we are connected beyond the flesh (this body is just a trap anyway) and that we always will be. We just move to another place/level/existence after this reality/world/life. As I write this, I still cannot find the right words to describe my certainty of this. But I know this, I will see my girl again—10,000% sure. And everyone who has lost someone will see their loved one again—it is a promise. But as long as we are still here—we need to live our best and most fearless lives. Again, the words I am typing do not do justice to what I want to convey. I want others to feel the comfort and certainty that I feel. I know not everyone wants or is ready to hear or believe this—but it is my truth.

Finally, I share this detailed account because I know how doubt can linger in our hearts and minds surrounding our loved ones and the afterlife. Here is what happened to Stevie, who gave permission to share her story here:

When I was 14 years old, my little brother Dakota, who was nine years old, passed away from sudden cardiac arrest three days after his first heart surgery. My little brother and I inherited some genetic heart defects from our Dad's side and a blood clotting disorder that we both struggled with our whole lives. His passing-away anniversary is just over a week away, and every year it's quite sad for my Dad and me.

I feel guilty all the time that, despite having the same heart conditions and the same heart surgery, I've made it to 25 years old and now have two children of my own, but he never made it past nine years old. Watching my Dad mourn his only son's death every year is an anguish that words can't fully describe.

Two weeks ago, I told my four-year-old son that we were heading to North Dakota for the weekend and my son got excited and said, "I played with him at Grandma's!" I've never told my children about Dakota and have a hard time talking about him. It startled me that my son said that he played with a Dakota, because this is a small town and no boys have that name here. I didn't mention it to anyone but I started meditating every evening, trying to reach out to my brother.

We've had things happen before over the past 11 years, like sometimes thinking that I could hear him laughing or (even before I had my son), we would randomly find his Hot Wheels cars around my dad's house, that he keeps up in a display case with Dakota's ashes and other things, or the TV turning on and it being his favorite cartoon show playing.

Unfortunately, last year in June, I also had my second miscarriage, and it still stings my heart. These past few weeks have been a struggle with all this on my heart, wanting the chance to say goodbye to my little brother and closure about my miscarriages.

And then I saw him last night in my dream and it felt so real. I was sleeping and then suddenly I was 'awake.' But I was in his room at my dad's house (over 1,000 miles away!). I heard him call my name and then he walked right into the room. He sat on the floor near my feet and pulled a couple Hot Wheels cars out of his pocket and started playing with them. We never actually talked with our mouths, but we could still hear each other. He smiled (still missing one of his baby teeth), and started talking about how much fun he's been having and the people he's met.

He told me he talked to a man who said he knew me, that I had helped him, and that his name was Dan. And that happens to be the name of the first person who passed away while I was trying to save them. I'm a paramedic. And my little brother is the whole reason I pursued my career in assisting people and trying to save lives.

Then he got up and hugged me, and it felt so amazing. I could feel his little body against mine. I could smell him. Everything was like it was real, and I haven't felt that in 11 years, so I couldn't stop myself from beginning to cry. I swear, I would've never let go of him, but then Dakota said he was supposed to show me something.

He then stepped back and did something I can't properly describe in words, but I have to try. He told me to close my eyes and so I did. But when I closed my eyes I could still see and hear him, but we weren't in his room anymore, we were somewhere that I couldn't see with my eyes, but something inside me knew I'd been there before. Then he cupped his two hands over his heart for a second and then threw them out and the two most beautiful, shimmering lights appeared, and started gently bouncing around us and softly touching us. They were so mesmerizing, I can't comprehend just how breathtakingly beautiful these two little lights dancing around were. And then suddenly I just knew that these two little lights were my two babies I'd lost. He told me that he plays with them and teaches them, when they come to see him, and they tell him about the lives they live now somewhere else.

I was totally blown away by it all. Then Dakota told me it was time for me to go because (my two children) needed me back. He knew my two living children by name! The two little lights came back between us and then disappeared and then instantly we were back in his room again. We hugged each other and I told him that I missed him and then we said goodbye. And when I woke up this morning I found the small ambulance Hot Wheels car that I keep in memory of him sitting on my nightstand, instead of the shelf I keep it on in the living room.

I really truly believe that I saw my little brother and my

two unborn babies last night, and I feel like I can finally be at peace now with my losses. It still makes me sad, but I know this experience will let me move on and let go of the pain.

Life after death is a mysterious and beautiful experience. Thank you so much to anyone who read my experience. Wishing you all the best.

may we consider that our deceased loved ones carried an eternal love inside them that we are able to reconnect with at any moment in time

may we open ourselves to recognize when we may be receiving signs or communication from our loved ones

as much as we miss their feet on the planet, may we rest in the comfort that love never dies

transformation:
death becomes you

one day you find

the stardust within

the purest essence

of all that is

and ever will be

you hold it gently

within the precious space

you create

where it echoes of

your sacredness

and rest

in the knowing

you were carried by love

into this life

and it will be love

that carries you home

to those waiting patiently

for your return

until then

simply

be

After speaking with so many people about their experiences surrounding death, I've come to the conclusion that one of the reasons for our overwhelming societal tendency to stuff our feelings and stories about grief and death is because we are so numbed by our initial shock and the intensity of the feelings of love and loss.

We are afraid of what will become of us if we release these deep feelings and allow those sentiments to speak up and explore and wander into the world.

Friends and loved ones can be afraid of that, too.

Ultimately their awkward placations and messages of *move on* grow from an overwhelming fear of losing you as well, for when we are in that startled place after loss, we cannot bear to consider further casualties.

Everyone within our loss bubble feels at least a hint of the intensity, likely sensing the deep griever's feet occasionally floating just a bit off the ground, and they cannot consider that you might float away as you cling to that string of deep love and loss.

What those people do not realize is that, for most of us, that string that connects to our loved one is what is keeping us alive.

When emotional responses to our grief are buried, the band-aid responses can only do so much.

On the surface, you may seem to suffer less, or your people may feel better because you seem to be moving on, ever so gracefully. But what we know from repeated conversations with survivors is that resentment over not feeling understood can then grow with your grief.

Not feeling validated or being misunderstood or continually stuffing our feelings can feed an angry fire, built from that repression, that can seep out into other areas of our lives.

We have a deep natural need for connection, to be understood, and when people who have experienced a loved one's death put on a smile and singsong *I'm fine* voice, resentment can lie beneath.

Resentment that people would even expect or accept an answer of *I'm fine*.

Resentment about the fact people don't talk or ask about your loved one or trauma or loss anymore.

Resentment that the message implicit in that silence is that what you are going through doesn't matter enough to unpack and process.

Resentment about superficial interactions you no longer want to take part in.

Resentment that there is no way to share the glimpses of magic you are seeing and feeling because you fear that these well-meaning, supportive individuals will question your sanity.

Resentment that you are left with feelings of isolation, anger at being abandoned, being misunderstood, feeling marginalized, heartbroken that others are no longer honoring your loved one … and the list goes on.

While we have a large population who, after a loss, choose the road less felt, many people are simply unable to choose that path and must grieve openly, processing what happened, and what death has done with them, and must live in a way that honors their deceased people.

Is there an in-between?

It seems that the intensity of the bond with the person who died and the foundation of that relationship directly correlate with how much the person's death becomes a part of one's everyday living.

Parents do not just say goodbye to their deceased children—they think of them constantly, love them, miss and mourn them, and have chosen ways to honor them within their lives and their families.

Fortunately, we hear fewer and fewer stories like the one I shared at the beginning of this book, where all signs of the child are erased and their name is never again spoken.

Any of you who, after deep loss, have chosen to feel your feelings and be open to your cognitive and emotional terrain may recall the turns in the road where you could identify, viscerally, how your loved one's death was redefining your living and the way you walked in the world.

As hard as that process can be, it's even harder to walk blindfolded, stumbling and falling, when we feel our emotional foundation shaking and trembling beneath us. When we feel crevices forming that make our walking more treacherous and disjointed. When what previously held us up is forever changed. Trying to hide from death and grief, we may find we can't put our finger on the *why* of it all because we have blocked ourselves from exploring how deeply death has had its way with us, our changed-ness, something we've never really learned about in the context of death and grief.

Within the project, I'm occasionally asked to share or speak. Typically, I'm asked to provide a bio. I have often written that the death of my soul-connects took me apart, dismantled me, and that now I'm put together differently. Such an infantile description, really, but it illustrates my transformation as succinctly as I can.

As mentioned previously, I believe that your trauma and grief can change you on a cellular level.

Everything changes. The way you sleep, the way you eat, the way you breathe, the way you feel. And it's impossible to believe that these changes don't affect your very essence, transforming every aspect of you.

These deep changes also occur after births, partnering, other times of beauty and tragedy; thus is the essence of our walk through this life.

I'm aghast that anything about grieving can be turned into a *disorder*.

181

Yes, if you have an underlying autonomic system that organically revs, creating anxiety-type symptoms or a history of depression, certainly bereavement can serve as kindling and fuel your symptom-thinking. But the idea of turning grief into an abnormality serves no one and creates even further invalidation and disconnection.

Consider finding a partner to accompany you through your transformation. I believe the life experience of intimately dealing with the death of an essential relationship is necessary for a professional to effectively sit with you while you negotiate your own experience with death and dying. (You will find some listed at the end of this book and you can listen to their stories.)

And I fully understand that people in the helping field who read this may think, *hmm, I can still be an effective listener,* and won't fully understand this viewpoint until their time with the death of a primary person in their life arrives.

Do not be intimidated by the process of attempting to find the best professional fit; it is smart and helpful to interview someone with whom you expect to share your inner workings.

Another guideline for after you have found that person is to give it three sessions before you decide the person isn't for you, unless something so troubling occurs earlier that you cannot return. The soothing balm of knowing you are not alone can be tremendously healing and empowering.

As you move forward in your own life, you will carry the memory and love of your deceased person with you.

At first it might feel utterly impossible.

Strangely, after my brother and mom's death, I got on a kick of reading extreme survival stories. I read an account of the first woman to traverse Antarctica alone, on foot. She spoke of packing into the tent every night, and as the sun rose, the dread of continuing rose in her as well. Knowing she was returning to the desolate and blinding expanse and bitter cold, she had to muster the psychic and physical energy to keep going. Her morning mantra became: *Just get out of the tent.*

Many times since reading that book I have told myself: *Just get out of the tent. Go through the motions, meet your obligations.* All while fully knowing that my emotional self would prefer to stay snuggled in, away from the world.

More recently I've adapted the mantra of *look forward.* As we talked about earlier, the aftermath of death and time of grieving can hold up a gigantic rear-view mirror where we question our past actions.

How much headspace do you think you devote to going over your regrets and *should-haves*?

Yes, it's important to adequately process the situation, our history, and all that goes with that, but there came a time when I realized that I was better served spending my time in the present moment and looking towards tomorrow rather than dwelling in the past. As we drive forward, we are only meant to glance in the rear-view mirror now and then. If we lock our gaze onto what is behind us, we will have an accident, hurting ourselves and maybe others.

It's a hard call, because the past is where we find images of our loved ones, still living, but if you can feel connection with your person in the great beyond, understanding that energy never dies, it becomes easier to look forward and connect with what remains of them: love.

There will be a day, if you process your emotions with heart wide open, that the bell of transformation will begin to ring, occasionally.

It will signal moments when you recognize your joy and grief coexisting. Herald when your creativity is reemerging. Find you making choices about how you want to move forward in the world. See you carrying the legacy of your loved one in your heart, and sometimes, building something beautiful from that. Opening up to synchronicity and letting in glimpses of magic and connection to your loved one.

Maybe it's best we release the goal of returning to the person we were pre-loss. Maybe that return to business as usual is absolutely impossible. Maybe we start to feel sparks of excitement about our precious life.

If you are reading this as a griever, it may feel impossible to move past the acute pain you are experiencing now.

An exercise of trust is necessary. Trusting that you can show up to your loss and grief and that, by letting it wash over you, there will be life anew.

May you go well and in peace, and may the greater good lead your process.

tales of transformation

As you walk the terrain of keeping your feet on the planet after your loved one has died, if you seek others who have walked that walk before you, you may find their stories comforting and inspiring.

An observation heard repeatedly, and experienced within myself, is a lower tolerance for idle chitchat and focusing too much on mundane things. Opening to full-spectrum living changes one's style of communication, so that you prefer to connect with people on a deeper level. Many find it difficult to find those people in their day-to-day lives.

One blessing for my tender, grieving heart has been the people I have connected with through *The Death Dialogues Project*.

When I hear their stories, a part of my heart exhales, and although the differences in our circumstances may be quite stark, we are connected by the thread of understanding of deep loss.

The brave and generous people who have shared their stories for this project are beautiful souls who will welcome you to their world.

They are your people.

In the following words you will find the answer some of those folks gave to the question: *How has your grief or death transformed you?*

How are my footsteps different as a result of loss, most specifically the death of my husband? I have learned that grief and joy are opposites and can be carried indefinitely, at the same time. Sometimes they are heavy and sometimes not. I have the ability to shed things that do not serve me, so that I expand rather than contract. I am even more comfortable in the grey zones, in the spaces where souls don't need bodies or voices to communicate. As Anita Moorjani notes, there are no coincidences. So a katydid on my living room wall has something very specific to say, as does the picture in my social media feed or the song that comes up in my playlist. And the more I open to what I can carry and how the world speaks in many dimensions, the more I revel in my own path.

Jana Buhlmann, whose husband chose MAID (medical assistance in dying) on September 25, 2017

www.bringthejoy.blog

Hear her in-depth story on Episodes 11 and 12 of *The Death Dialogues Project Podcast.*

It's hard for me to identify the transformation I've experienced due to the loss of my son three years ago. I know I've changed, but it's difficult to know if it's always been my character and an inevitable path, or if the changes are a direct result from grief. Something grief has forced upon me in a rather unexpected way is becoming much more selective with the people with whom I surround myself and my family. Additionally, starting the nonprofit has elevated this. I have always felt a sense of leadership, but now I am identified as one. And with this new role comes great responsibility. Bad company ruins good morals. And we who grieve are much more vulnerable than before. So extra caution in the area of whom we trust has now become essential.

Kjerstin Davies
Co-Founder + President
Charlie's Guys
www.charliesguys.org
Hear more of Kjerstin's story on Episode 29 of *The Death Dialogues Project Podcast.*

In 2015, four of my friends died in unrelated, unexpected tragedies. At first, I was overcome with terror that death was around every corner, waiting for me, too. Then, I realized the most important truth of my life: I have absolutely no control over when or how I die––but I have complete control over how I live until that mystery moment comes. The truth that I might die tomorrow has made me come alive. It keeps me in the now and it makes me feel free to be the most me. Above all, I'm just so happy to be alive today.

Kate Manser
Founder of YOU MIGHT DIE TOMORROW
Author of *You Might Die Tomorrow*
www.youmightdietomorrow.com
Hear more of Kate's story on Episode 30 and 113 of *The Death Dialogues Project Podcast.*

Being with loss is being with life. After experiencing the sudden death of my mother in 1993, I believe it was no accident that I continued to meet women who had also experienced mother loss. I am certain the universe put them in my orbit for a reason. I feel like a North Star or magnet of sorts in and around those who have experienced grief. The Memory Circle was born as a way to broaden or formalize this connection. To take death and the way we share our stories from hushed tones to a space of sharing.

Our stories must be witnessed and heard to make meaning of them. I imagined a place and space to sit shoulder-to-shoulder in community, where people mourning loss of all kinds, in a variety of settings and incarnations including writing work, meditation, intuitive medium sessions, healing yoga and more could help change the vernacular around grief and make space for it—quite literally. We can honor ourselves and our grief by sharing our stories and tales so that it may become more open and accepted. It has been transformational and felt quite on purpose to be working in this space. Death touches us all. We need to celebrate a life gone, as we do those who remain without them. Making new memories for a new time.

Barri Leiner Grant
@thememorycircle
Chief Grief Officer
www.thememorycircle.com
Listen to Barri's story on Episode 76 of *The Death Dialogues Project Podcast*.

I remember very clearly the morning my soul sister and best friend died. After an extended illness, her death did not come as a surprise; rather as the end of a long, sad goodbye. As the reality superficially sank in, I still felt her close. It snowed that morning, which was strange for March weather in Ohio. The snowflakes danced as they fell and were larger and sparklier than ever before. It seemed the birds paused and smiled at me, the flowers appeared more colorful. All of it a sign, that she was okay and still a part of this big world.

Her death has changed me and made me realize that there is no getting over death and loss, no moving on, rather a slow, beautiful moving forward, where you carry your loved one with you in a different form. Today, in this life after the death of my friend, all that I do and all that I am is, in part, a remembrance of her. There is beauty here on the other side of death, but there is sadness and loss too. My friend is where she always was, in my heart, and there she will remain.

Emily Holody

Find me on Facebook at: Emily Hampshire-Holody or on my blog at:

https://storiesfromasoulsister.wordpress.com/author/storiesfromasoulsister/

You can hear more of Emily's story on Episode 19 of *The Death Dialogues Project Podcast.*

"Sometimes you can't know, until you know." Until the first morning after my mother's death I had no idea how I would manage to live without the one person that had always been there for me. And then there was no choice. My heart broke a million times over, and yet I became a little more fearless. If I could realize and survive one of my worst fears, I was stronger than I ever knew. It gave me the courage to move my young family overseas for six years and travel the world. The final conversations I had with my mum that were sad, funny and practical, gave me endless comfort and revealed a passion to encourage others to talk about what is important to them. I didn't "get over" Mum dying, but I was and continue to be able to move forward because of her and all that she was and taught me. I choose to believe she is always with me. I still have her perfumes and apply her bright lipsticks. And each day I look at her ring that now sits on my finger, and it reminds me that the world continues to turn just like she said it would.

Kellie Curtain
Author: *What will I wear to your funeral?*
Hear more of Kellie's story on Episode 89 of *The Death Dialogues Project Podcast.*

I was 14 the first time I was in the room when someone died—and the process of death was traumatizing for the immediate family because no one was talking about the toxic family secrets or acknowl-edging these dynamics. For me, this distorted grief and connection was painfully difficult to witness. As time went on, I recognized that we often miss what we most need when we are grieving: community, honesty, healthy boundaries, and compassion for both ourselves and those around us. I am naturally drawn to problem solving, and I recognized that there must be social and cultural changes in the way we both understand and communicate with each other about death, grief and dying. To this end I was inspired to write and create an inclusive online end-of-life training course that emphasizes the importance of language and communication style, listening, and comprehensive understanding of all seven non-medical roles. The more we understand and share, the better we can connect—this was the part of grief that transformed my life.

Dr. Annetta Mallon
End of life consultant and educator
Affiliation: Gentle Death Education and Planning
https://gdep.teachable.com/ https://www.gdep.com.au
You can listen to Annetta on Episode 81 of *The Death Dialogues Project Podcast*.

My husband Jacques Thiroux died in 2006. I was sure I would never love again, until I met my next husband, Rev. Ron Threatt. Both men were brilliant, kind, and full of love. After Ron died, I was lost. Sharing my life with both of them was what I lived for, and when they were gone, I started questioning what I was supposed to be doing. The answer came when Ron's dear friend died suddenly. I reached out to his wife to share what I had learned that I knew could help her. The more I wrote to her, the more I realized I could use my writing to help others. I found lots of ways to help, starting with people I knew, then creating online classes and private Facebook groups, and ultimately writing a book. Finding this purpose has transformed me and has given me the opportunity to speak at retreats and be interviewed online as well as having a thriving online community. I am grateful to have discovered my path serving others and helping me with my own grief in the process.

Emily Thiroux Threatt
Author of *Loving and Living Your Way Through Grief*
www.lovingandlivingyourwaythroughgrief.com
You can hear more of Emily's story on Episode 85 of The Death Dialogues Project Podcast.

At the age of 10, I had to learn the hardest lesson of all: people you love, die.

When my dad died, my heart was broken into two pieces. In between those two pieces grew bravery and compassion. I learned that while life can crumble, it is the "crumble" that just might become your greatest strength.

I have brought that little 10-year-old heart along with me, as I have journeyed through my life. I've learned that grief does not leave your body, heart, or mind. Please, never let anyone tell you that it should.

I have also learned that when someone you love dies, your heart stops. Not literally, of course, but the way it knew how to beat and pump and help you to live your life … all changes. It can never be the same.

But I have also learned about empathy, pain and love. And hope. And life. And living. And resilience.

I will never be grateful for or see the beauty in my dad's death. I am, however, grateful to understand that my sadness is okay. My joy is okay, too. Feeling both at the same time means I have loved and felt loved.

I know for sure that the jagged edges of your healing heart is the space where the memories of someone you have loved find their way in. I have spent years teaching people about grief, remembering, honoring and connecting.

And with every ounce of my being, it has been my honor and privilege.

Randi Pearlman Wolfson
Grief and Grits on Facebook/Instagram
"Eddie's Brave Journey: How one little elephant learned all about grief"
www.EddiesBraveJourney.com
Hear more of Randi's story on Episode 78 of *The Death Dialogues Project Podcast.*

Since my husband's death in January 2018, the biggest transformation that I have undergone is my belief in myself. Around the second anniversary of his passing, I realized that I did things that were hard. In the beginning it was just getting out of bed. Next it was going back to work. Then it was selling our home and living on my own for the first time ever. Finally, I decided to get my life coaching certification to help other widows. The training was intense, to say the least. But the point of it was to make us look deep within ourselves the same way we want our clients to look, in order to get real, life-changing results. Because of the training, I realized that I am a strong and resilient woman. My confidence has grown by leaps and bounds. I trust myself, my intuition and my decisions. I know that I am capable of making the best choices for myself on my own. This is the most secure I have ever felt in my entire life.

Stephanie Sprinkel
Instagram @survivingtheloss & @chooseyourselfcoaching
You can hear Stephanie speaking after her husband died on Episode 5 and hear her speak of further transformation on Episode 63 of *The Death Dialogues Project Podcast.*

Four a.m. this morning, Aunt Madeline woke me up with smiles. I think of Uncle George, who came to me after his death. Policeman Harry was the first to arrive. Older brother Andrew answered my prayer. My son Shannon, who died, is at peace with these dead people.

Shannon inspires his Pops to begin and end each day with prayer, thanksgiving, and to share gratitude. He went home to guide his dad through the trail of life. No more tears. Heaven knows Pops needs the help.

Sunrise and sunset thanksgivings open for the deceased and the living. I lay acceptance and humility in my creator's hands. Give me strength, beauty, and the love to help, I say once more.

Someday, my son will arrive to retrieve his dad. I am ready.

In the meantime, Shannon, watch over Pops and the family. Come to Pops.

Miigwetch—thank you, son. I miss you so much. Love, Pops.

Kenn Pitawanakwat, author of *When My Son Died*
Kenn is of the Odawa, Pottawatomi, Ojibwe confederacy
www.kennpitawanakwat.com
Hear Kenn's story on Episode 26 of *The Death Dialogues Project Podcast.*

In the States, we have been programmed by capitalism, a rigid machine with productivity as the goal, rather than living lives full of that which brings us meaning and joy. When I have the privilege of being with dying people, with time to reflect on their lives, I get to hear about the things that remain important into the end of their lives. I have learned to try to live my life fully, feeling with all six of my senses, as often as I can. It is in these moments that loss has transformed, in fractal fashion, my life, movements, learnings, family, friends, views, desires, and passions.

Lashanna Williams
Antares Wellness
antareswellness.com
Hear more from Lashanna on Episode 58 of *The Death Dialogues Project Podcast.*

At the split moment I was told my son, Nanda, was dead, the part of myself I called "Me" vanished. I began falling, trying to make sense of something that makes no sense, yearning for the impossible—for my son to be alive. I flailed, grasping, fully engaged in the unsolvable maze of grief. Before the anniversary of my son's passing, sorrow sank its roots into me, and with nothing left to lose, I leaned in to do whatever it took to face the death of my boy, to heal. I have always been a doer, a hard worker—I assumed I would be able to work my loss out. But in my agony, I soon found that it didn't require a lot of work; no, it required an enormous amount of being. Being in the unknown, groundless, being uncomfortable, in deep pain, being unsure, fearful, crazy, being out of control, powerless, unable, being judged, misunderstood, dismissed, being angry, being hateful, loveless, numb, being frail, vulnerable, suicidal, being in denial, being in truth, being on a merry-go-round to repeat everything over and over, but also being forced open, sensitive and aware, but most importantly, being new. Grief offered itself in abundance, and there was no turning it down. I, being alone, on that unstoppable train, decided to take notes—ask questions. I danced with grief, carved what I knew, painted the details, drew my insides out, and wrote my story until I became the grief artist, the grief expert, engaged in the fine art of grieving—my new way of seeing. Loss changes as life changes. And in all my being, my ever so enormously being, the engine of grief eventually idled and then ceased. I discovered my new relationship to Nanda, to who I was, who we were, and who I am now, in a life worth living.

Jane Edberg
https://www.thefineartofgrieving.com/
https://www.instagram.com/thefineartofgrieving/?hl=en
https://www.facebook.com/thefineartofgrieving/
Hear more of Jane's story on Episode 43 of *The Death Dialogues Project Podcast*.

Losing my mom as an infant changed me in ways I'll never fully realize, because I didn't get the opportunity to even know who I am without grief in my life. But living with lifelong grief has also given me a unique perspective about what the world believes and expects surrounding grief and loss.

For a long time, I felt isolated, invisible, and alone, because most of what I'd been told about bereavement simply wasn't true (for me). After years of struggling, I finally stopped trying to force myself into a box and gave myself permission to ignore society's unrealistic expectations. I started grieving my own way, and that alone has been the biggest turning point in my grief journey.

Lindsay Joy Taylor
Owner, The Joyful Jewelry Box
updates and grief support: https://www.bit.ly/tjjbnews
https://www.instagram.com/TheJoyfulJewelryBox
https://www.TheJoyfulJewelryBox.com
Listen to Lindsay's story on Episode 56 of *The Death Dialogues Project Podcast.*

I emerged from my year of grief—my baptism into it—as a better, softer human. (Just that little thing!) As I trudged and healed, I became brave enough to sit with grief and no longer step over mine or anyone else's in a pursuit of relentlessly being upright and "okay," as I had so often in the past. I will forever contend that grief is one of the great loves of my life, and it is largely because knowing it and walking with it has let me live in robust, sweet relationship with all the facets of my life. Grief drove me to step fully into what feels like a calling, to guide others to be better at grief, too. I've learned that not only is grief inevitable, it's also all around us all the time, and I consider it a life skill to support our fellow humans in it.

Tara Caffelle, writer and grief consultant
Website: www.thisisgriefatwork.com
Listen to Tara's story on Episode 87 of *The Death Dialogues Project Podcast.*

My walk with grief and loss has been the most transformative journey of my life. I know that I am more mindful, open-hearted and compassionate because of the griefs I hold, and of course they've led me to my work as a grief coach and death midwife. But among the gifts I never expected was the courage I've grown into. Saying goodbye to my dad, a year after losing a longtime father figure in my life, was the hardest thing I had to do. I made so many challenging, bold and unexpected decisions in the years after that loss, from leaving a relationship to ending a career. With each one, no matter how daunting, I felt that if I had already done the singular most difficult thing I'd ever had to do, then I could do this, too. Every one of those decisions, which included the pursuit of a long-held dream, was anchored in a bravery I never would have cultivated had I not been at my dad's bedside in the final days of his life.

Naila Francis
Naila is a grief coach and death midwife. You can find her at www.thishallowedwilderness.com
You can hear more of Naila's story on Episode 84 of *The Death Dialogues Project Podcast.*

My grief is the path I walk to my true self. My dad's death splintered me open in a way that I needed to be shattered. It cracked apart all the unyielding, ingrained beliefs that I was holding onto, and when those filtered away, I could see life differently. I began to see that we are not merely human beings with a connection to the divine, nor are we divine beings simply having a human experience. Our humanness and our holiness are one and the same. I live from this frame of reference. Grief came not simply as an emotion, but an expansive encounter of the range of my emotions. Some pop up briefly and startle me, some gently rock me, some come screaming out, and some run like a current underneath everything else. Grief unlocked me to all of my emotions, and I live now knowing that everything I experience is sacred. The loss of my dad opened me up to a new view of humanity, a different understanding of love, and deeper compassion. I cry harder and I laugh louder. It has been the most painful and most beautiful thing I've ever experienced.

Rev. Melissa Harris, M.S., M.Div.
@woh.mod (Where Humanity Meets Divinity)
Hear more from Melissa on Episode 34 of *The Death Dialogues Project Podcast.*

The most important thing I have learned is that being happy after loss is about letting go. When my life went off script, I had to let go of my beliefs around what my life would look like for the next 30 years or so. This was not easy, but slotting a new character into an old slot was not a workable option for me. I tried. Loss taught me that death comes for all of us, and that it will come for me. With this in mind, I knew that I wanted to write my own next chapters rather than to follow some slightly altered version that failed to take this juicy tidbit of information into consideration. To let go meant I had to have enough faith that walking into a space I could not yet see was better than pretending we get all the time we want to be here. This shifted living in today to the forefront of how I live, and it's reduced the control "someday" holds over me. To live this way is liberating, and I am again happy. It is a different happy but to get here, I had to let go of the old happy. Do not be afraid to let go of what no longer makes sense and search out what may. Be brave.

Heike Mertins, Author
Grief is … Thoughts on loss, struggle and new beginnings
W: heikemertins.com
B: heikemertins.com/blog
Hear more of Heike's story on Episode 22 of *The Death Dialogues Project Podcast.*

I was initiated into a life path of apprenticing to grief; thrust through the gateway of ecological despair and spiritual grief. In my twenties, this pain culminated in an immobilized state of wrenching heartache for the disruptions in our humanity that take so many guises. I felt alone in this, powerless, and without community or rituals to support this threshold. But from this painful experience, I have learned that our grief isn't what needs healing. Rather, our healing needs our grief. This is a guiding beacon for me, and I am committed to reclaiming intimacy with grief in personally and culturally relevant ways, through the realms of therapeutic, ancestral and ritual grief support. I do this because I experienced the deep disservice it does to life, to self, to relationships, to be disconnected from my grief and from holistic ways of being with my grief. Grief brought me back to myself, so I could (and can) live the transformation that it invites. To me, grief is an expression of radical love, resilience, and transformative power towards personal and collective healing. I am devoted to living this vision the best I can.

Shauna Janz – Sacred Grief
www.sacredgrief.com
Hear Shauna's story on Episode 68 of *The Death Dialogues Project Podcast.*

Making space for grief has sweetened life and deepened connection. Loss has emptied me in a way that means in the recovery I have sifted and sorted and become clearer in my desires and purpose in ways that mean I am more alive and more true.

Jane Cunningham
www.gentle-conversations.com
@numinousjane
Listen to more of Jane's experience on Episode 16 of *The Death Dialogues Project Podcast*.

When I think about how grief has transformed me, I see two pictures of myself: Before-Loss-Sandy and After-Loss-Sandy. They are different people.

Oh yes, I've transformed. Everything has changed. My view of the world has shifted. There is very little that is the same.

Broadly speaking—I (mind-body-spirit "I") have become bigger and smaller simultaneously. I do not feel, nor believe, that transformation means change only towards the better. For I have felt shifts the other way, too.

I have lost my innocence—something I still grieve to this day. I gained maturity— emotional and spiritual maturity, which has revealed a well of compassion for myself and others on a whole new level. I was always a compassionate person, but now it's different. It's felt, embodied and informs how I live my life.

This maturity harbors fear about how quickly life can change. It knows the reality that death will come to all of us, as will grief. I always held a deep appreciation for each day, but now, there's a layer of worry, about anything and everything that could happen. Anxiety has become my sidekick.

My transformation includes learning how to live like this—with a heart broken open. How to cope with ALL of it—the good and the bad. Considering it all, I've metamorphosed into someone who is at home in her own skin, even when it's on fire with sorrow or anger. I have felt renewal in my grief—where it is not the enemy, or something to be banished, but a very important part of who I am. I am more aligned and in-line with myself.

I have new eyes and a new heart. Due to this inner revolution, I had to make changes in how I saw people supported in grief. I couldn't look away. My vocation changed to include work in the areas of end-of-life and grief support.

When I picked up the pieces of my life after Cam, my partner, died, how I put them back together was different. That's transformation. And, curiously, as I write this 14 years later, that loss, and losses that have happened since, have continually transformed and changed me.

Sandy Ayre
www.yogaforgriefsupport.com
You can hear Sandy's story on Episode 10 of *The Death Dialogues Project Podcast.*

Death changes people. For me, death flipped my world upside down. I had lost a few grandparents before my mom died and then, boom—I transformed into "my mom." Taking care of all things she would have done or needed to do. It was like a switch went off in my body. I now know, being 20 years removed from her death, that my time on earth now is to help others through their grief. Her death brought out my soul's passion to help those who grieve, even though I'm grieving myself.

We all grieve differently and also grieve differently for each person that dies that we are close to. Choosing to live my life through my mom, and now dad, who recently passed, is how I get through each day.

Tom Biddulph
goodgrievings.com
@goodgrievings
Hear Tom's story on Episode 73 of *The Death Dialogues Project Podcast.*

When I think of how my grief over the loss of our two-month-old daughter has transformed me, it's hard to put into words. I feel like life will forever be divided into "before" and "after" Emily. I have found that I am a much more compassionate and empathetic person, particularly in cases of similar loss. Before, I would just be a little sad for others, but now I feel their pain deep in my heart, much like when my own loss happened. Because of this I feel compelled to do more to help. I hope to one day become a bereavement doula and help other families walk this path. I feel like this not only helps me find meaning in my own loss but is also a way to honor my Emily's memory.

I have also discovered that my perspective on life and time has changed dramatically. I am now keenly aware of how fleeting life is and have learned to appreciate the little moments which can turn out to be big moments. Most people fear death, but as a bereaved mother, knowing my baby is waiting on the other side of this life has completely removed any fear of death. I'm not saying I want to die, just that whenever it happens, I am at peace about it.

Chris Frazier
Hear Chris's story on Episode 36 of *The Death Dialogues Project Podcast.*

The sudden death of my father was the first significant death in my life. It was a dream that transformed my grief. In my dream, I walked up to my father and said that I loved him and that I would miss him (acknowledging his death). We hugged, and then I woke up. When I woke up, my grief had changed and my love of grief dreams was born. A few years later, I began to research these types of dreams in my MA and PhD. I now raise awareness on grief dreams all over the world. I could have never imagined that the death of my father would have brought me here.

Dr. Joshua Black (www.GriefDreams.ca)
Listen to Joshua's story on Episode 62 of *The Death Dialogues Project Podcast.*

When my mother, Irobel Herring, died in 2001, I learned to co-create with nature and with death, in a way that informed and transformed my life and how I view mortality, loss and the anguish and grief we feel when someone or something that we love dies. I am still exploring, still learning what such co-creation means. This inquiry set up house in my heart and being, like a koan or mantra, inspiring and guiding my life. It has led me to work in the field of death and dying, as a home funeral and green burial guide, and as a "green" licensed funeral director. It has inspired me to bring families and communities more natural and healing ways to care for our loved ones after death— in ways that care for the earth and the natural world as well. I have written a book and narrated an audiobook called *Reimagining Death: Stories and Practical Wisdom for Home Funerals and Green Burials*, which contains the story of my mother's remarkable transition. Nature, life and death are my sacred teachers now. I am less fearful as a human being and more grateful to be alive.

Lucinda Herring
www.lucindaherring.com
https://www.facebook.com/ReimaginingDeathBook
Hear more from Lucinda on Episode 17 of *The Death Dialogues Project Podcast.*

I would be lying to say I am not often nostalgic for the person I was before I experienced traumatic losses. Traumatic because they were not losses that speak to the circle of time, but more of the sudden, unfair fragility of life. (Living with that fragility is a bit like stepping through the looking glass and finding a whole different version of you exists. The life you imagined will not happen; a different life will, and that can go on in its ability to change at a moment's notice endlessly.) I miss the "her" I used to feel confident in calling "myself;" her self-assuredness, her more often than not light-heartedness, her bright hope-filled face; and in some ways I miss the not-knowing. It is not because that person hadn't experienced hard things prior to loss, but more so because she had and was still able to carry hope, security and possibility with her in abundance. I feel now loss has aged me in a way that adds weight behind my eyes; loss has made me need more calm and quiet so I can listen and hear better. Most importantly, and perhaps profoundly, loss has made me understand gravity better. Gravity of the soul, lightness of the body. It has made me walk around with a deep embodiment of joy and sadness and their parallel connection, their coexistence, as opposed to one existing only on the flipside of the other. That energetically—intense joy and intense sadness—they coexist; they dance alongside each other on the journey. That is the humanity of it, that is the compassion and empathy, the sinew of experience we all share. Understanding that coexistence deeper is what led me to create a body of work called "Your Faithful Reader." A call for space both in real time, performance, writing, reading, and witnessing for people's feelings and experiences to exist, be shared, carried, and let go of for the greater benefit of us all, seeing ourselves in others.

Making dance and theater, combined with working through my own grief, have taught me lessons in my life that I believe to be universal. One is how important it is to allow yourself to feel without shame; another is the immeasurable value of being a witness to someone else's experiences. As humans we are all connected through time, through stories; we find ways forward in moments both difficult and triumphant as a direct result of sharing and acknowledging that those experiences are valid. And in that our experiences can be someone else's survival guide, assuring them they are not alone.

Miriam Wasmund
You can find my work at www.yourfaithfulreader.com
@move2livenow @rememberinghenry and
@thegravelinmytravel
You can hear Miriam's story on Episode 90 of *The Death Dialogues Project Podcast.*

No one is the same person they were eleven years ago. I'm not the same person I was in January 2010, when my husband, Sean, died. I witnessed him near death in the ICU before he bounced back in rehabilitation hospitals and finally succumbed to surgical complications. It was a four-and-a-half-month slog of interventions, beeping, wires, tubes and tears.

Seeing how Sean's body was so quickly devastated crystallized for me the fact of life's brevity. Seven months after I lost my husband, the father of our four- and six-year-old children, I rented out our house, packed our bags and traveled the world for five months. Sean died while doing nothing more dangerous than driving or more exotic than hiking with small children. Postmortem, my risk tolerance increased. I tried paragliding for the first time. I took my kids to Europe, Africa, Australia and finally, to New Zealand.

I learned I was strong. And weak. Independent. And needy. Yet my biggest fear before our world tour was that I would settle into a new normal in my hometown and not explore.

I don't paraglide these days, but I did move to New Zealand. I love my life here. But I live with the knowledge everything can change in the instant. That's what death taught me.

Dawn Picken
Connect with me at my author page:
https://dawnpicken.com/author-page
Or on Instagram: @pickendawn
Hear more of Dawn's story on Episode 7 of *The Death Dialogues Project Podcast.*

Death is likely the most profound, transformative experience one can have. For me, the death of my mother changed me at my core. I am honest in saying it was equally the worst and best experience I've had. Though I was unable to say goodbye to her while she was in a conscious state, I had the privilege of watching her soul leave her body. It felt nothing like a privilege at the time, of course. It felt like time stopped. Suddenly, my mind and body, for the first time, were wholly present in the moment. The deep-rooted fear of my mother's death which I had had since childhood was staring me straight in the face. And yet, I survived. I feel utterly lucky to have experienced living through my biggest fear, because now I know I will always survive ... until my own demise, that is.

Kathryn Burns
You can hear Kathryn's story on Episode 93 of *The Death Dialogues Project Podcast*.

Death has transformed me in so many ways. It always does, whether we believe it or not. I felt broken when my husband took his life; that I couldn't possibly survive without him. What I saw as broken, at the time, was really broken *open*. Death and rebirth are linked for a reason. I didn't picture the life I have now at all. While I am still grieving quite profoundly, I have had adventures I would not have had, were he still here. Colors and music seem to be more deep and meaningful, and I feel a deep and abiding kinship with all of the grievers that I have met on this journey. I have a public account on Instagram to meet and connect with fellow widows and grievers. My handle is @jeniferbrd7761. I hope someday soon to be in a position to give real, solid assistance to widows. I am working on those details now.

Jenifer Davis
Listen to Jenifer on Episode 105 of *The Death Dialogues Project Podcast*.

Transformed by death

Until Mahyan died I was more familiar with birth than death, and I noticed how often my brain produced images of my heart that looked more like the jagged edges of a torn placenta than the shattered yet life-giving organ that would now pound and appear to beat out of time at random moments for years to come. After Mahyan died I felt bereft; physically aching for the loss of my son, only to discover fear had also come along for the ride as I realized the world where children were born, loved and raised to adulthood was no longer certain.

In what world had I previously felt this guarantee?

Death and the shattering of hearts and certainty is a transformative thing, right?

Gently tending to questions such as these has also transformed me; leaning greatly on the incredible and loving community around me, Mahyan's death has also brought connection; rivers of tears have become well-journeyed roads where those around me have nurtured, fed and sung to me and my family again and again. Close friends and colleagues have walked alongside and with my pain, shared stories and memories of Mahyan through many years, and I am transformed again as I notice my heart has a steadier pace, a peace amidst this mountain of grief. *The Death Dialogues Project* enabled a sharing of Mahyan's story; an opportunity to Say His Name; his life and his death. It was shattering and healing all at once, supported and lovingly midwifed, leaving me held and deeply connected to all who were present.

Madeleine Chaplin

Listen to Madeleine's story and a reading of the verbatim piece from our debut on Episode 97 of *The Death Dialogues Project Podcast.*

Taking care of someone at the end of life is different than taking care of someone who is going to get better. Most people don't know this. As a result of this lack of knowledge, the end-of-life process and care is judged by how people get better.

We, whose job it is to guide and support others during the dying process, fail the families *unless* we teach them the difference in end-of-life care.

Education, education, education, combined with support and guidance, can change a frightening experience into a sacred one. A sacred experience leads to a sacred memory. A sacred memory eases the grief of loss.

Barbara Karnes, RN
Barbara Karnes Books
End of Life Education Materials
BK books.com
You can hear more on Episode 107 of *The Death Dialogues Project Podcast.*

Death transformed me by turning up side-by-side with a deep sense of peace which was beyond my understanding.

My parents had been killed in a motor accident. My daughter, almost three, was traveling with them and was kept safe through a strange set of circumstances.

This is forty-odd years ago. I had never been afraid of death as a young person, especially not my own death, and this experience of death and peace walking together deepened my sense that death really is okay. That's not to say I didn't miss my parents, or find the next months easy—I did have to push myself through the chores of daily living, and often cried in the bath, but something deep in me knew that all was well.

This knowing informs my life in a very core way, and is reflected in my work and writing around death and dying.

Margaret McCallum
https://www.margaretmccallum.com/
Listen to Margaret's story on Episode 114 at *The Death Dialogues Project Podcast.*

Eleven years since the death of my Mum, I am now 26 and my perspective on death has evolved over the years. It has transformed from anger, confusion and loneliness to passion, love and empathy.

The fragility of life is so obvious to me, and although it took me eight-plus years and is always a work in progress, death has given me the opportunity to see the world, my experiences and my relationships through a new HD lens. It has created a way of connecting with people and taught me compassion—for both myself and others. I have clear values. I live in the moment, and I love deeply.

Death forced me to grow up quickly, and I can't say whether I'd be this person should my Mum still be alive. However, I am grateful for the opportunities I have received and that I may not have had the courage to pursue had I not seen death and the uncertainty of one more day at such a young age.

I can now say that death is a part of me—it molds my choices and it will always be there—but it does not define me.

Katrina Weller
Grief and Loss Educator and Advocate
www.katrinapreislerweller.com
Instagram: katrinalpweller
You can hear more on Episode 96 of *The Death Dialogues Project Podcast.*

This I know is true: if we are lucky enough to love, we are bound to mourn. Death is inevitable. I recently lost my husband, dad, and both brothers. It is a lot to bear, and I know I no longer am the person I was before. Surprisingly, I am evolving into a better version of myself.

Death has reminded me that our time in this world is limited, so I must seize the moments and cherish the mundane. It is the memories we leave behind that are the greatest gift for our loved ones. So, I am determined to continue saying yes to my friends and family and not sit back and watch life go by.

I also want to honor my loved ones.

Welcome to Code Blue—an annual day dedicated to end the taboo and open a dialogue about death. Let's educate and discuss all things death-related.

Join *evolve beyond grief* on the website, Facebook and Instagram.

Let's normalize death—before it kills you.

Susan Kendal
https://www.evolvebeyondgrief.com/
https://www.instagram.com/evolvebeyondgrief/
Listen to Susan's story on Episode 94 of *The Death Dialogues Project Podcast.*

The very brief life and death of my daughter, Madelyn Elizabeth, broke me to my very core. For years I was living my life just waiting to die. Until one day, I realized that my Maddie would not want me to be miserable—and making everyone around me miserable too. I realized I was at a crossroads: I could stay stuck in the bitter, allowing myself to only see the ugly and nasty in the world. Or, I could choose to be better, blooming into a happier, more loving, compassionate, and empathetic human being. You have that choice, too—and you'll know when it is time to make it. I hope you CHOOSE to be better, CHOOSE to find hope, and CHOOSE to love life again. Above all, I hope you always "Remember. You're not alone."

Crystal Webster
Madelyn's Mama and Founder of Sharing Solace
www.SharingSolace.com
Listen to Crystal's full story on Episode 103 of *The Death Dialogues Project Podcast*.

May you sense ease as you leave these stories, understanding that you are not alone in your experience or your pain.

May you find a peace in sitting with the beautiful-horrible of death, dying and its aftermath.

May your transformation be one of grace.

list of podcast episodes

You can find *The Death Dialogues Project Podcast* platforms at www.deathdialogues.net.

Podcast episodes are grouped by subject for quick reference.

Please note that each of these episodes touch on multiple areas; they have simply been grouped to help you quickly find episodes that are relevant to these topics, though other subjects will also be reflected in these episodes.

anticipatory grief

11 &12: Part One and Two: A Date with Death (assisted dying)

16. Jane Cunningham: Where Death has Taken Me; www.gentle-conversations.com

19. Loss of a Soul Sister: A Life Transformed

20. Rob Hamill: The Power of Ceremony & Symbolism

23. The Accidental Episode

36. Emily Elizabeth: She Changed Lives

38. Picture Death: A father's last 17 days are captured on film and a project is born

44. Reimagining Grief: Lisa Keefauver

48. After Chloe: The story

54. Walking Her Mother Home: Kristie Bennett

65. A Grief Warrior: Leslie Barber

74. Hope for Steve

grief

with grandfather)

87. Grief: A Love Story (multiple deaths)

85. Loving & Living Your Way Through Grief (two husbands & other deaths)

84. Awakened by Death: Naila Frances (father & mother's partner's deaths)

83. Wydowhood with Celeste (husband died quickly after cancer re-diagnosis and infant death)

82. The Long Walk Home: Find your Harbor (son died of brain cancer)

79. My Story of Stillbirth and Miscarriage: Amy Watson

78. The Heart of a Grieving Child: Grief & Grits (father when she was a child)

77. A Journey Without a Map: John Sardella (wife died of cancer)

76. The Memory Circle: Barri Leiner Grant (death of mother)

74. Hope for Steve (husband died after nine years of ALS)

73. Good Grievings: Thomas Biddulph (sixteen deaths since 1994, most recently father)

72. Our Lost Adventure: Bex Tingey (partner in paragliding acci-dent)

71. Grief Alchemy: Taurie Bednarski (sudden death of father)

67. Grieving Mothers: Meagan Hillukka (death of toddler)

66. Lysa Black: The Transformative Power of Death (miscarriage and death of horses)

65. A Grief Warrior: Leslie Barber (husband died of cancer)

63. Full Circle: Stephanie Sprinkel

62. Grief Dreams with Dr. Joshua Black (interest initiated with experience after death of his father)

56. Complex Trauma and Grief: Lindsay Joy Taylor (parent murdered when she was one year old)

54. Walking Her Mother Home: Kristie Bennett

50. Transforming Conversations: Aftermath of suicide in the workplace

51. Losing a Father at 12: An eloquent story of how death affects a child

48. After Chloe: The Story (infant and parental death)

47. Reframing Suicide: A mother's story (adult son ends his life)

46. A Grief Sublime: Beth Robbins (husband's sudden death)

44. Reimagining Grief: Lisa Keefauver (husband died of cancer)

43. The Fine Art of Grieving with Jane Edberg (young adult child)

42. Lessons from a Parent's Sudden Death (at 19 she had to be the primary survivor of father's death)

39. Medium Rebecca Rosen: Love & lessons from beyond

36. Emily Elizabeth: She changed lives (infant death)

34. Death & Divinity: Melissa Harris

32. Widowed at 30: Young mother of four negotiates life after loss (husband's sudden death)

31. Tricia Barker's Near Death Experience (NDE)

30. Kate Manser: You Might Die Tomorrow (changed by death)

29. Charlie's Guys: A wee boy's death brings gifts to grieving siblings

27. John Pavlovitz on Death & Grief (lessons after father's death)

26. Kenn Pitawanakwat: When My Son Died

24. To Die For: Listening to our hearts and whispers from the beyond

23. The Accidental Episode (wife's death from cancer/in-home vigil; recorded just months after her death)

22. Grief is ... with Heike Mertins (authored book after death of husband and brother)

21. Surviving Siblings: Kellyn Shoecraft (sibling death)

20. Rob Hamill: The power of ceremony & symbolism (NZ Olympian's brother was held captive & murdered by the Khmer Rouge)

19. Loss of a Soul Sister: A life transformed (soul sister & other family deaths)

18. Guided by Grief: Lisa Bovee (son killed in car accident)

10. Yoga & Grief: A match made in heaven (young partner death)

7. Traveling with Grief: A young widow's story (husband died of rare illness)

5. Grief & the Holidays (thoughts from a widow at first holiday time)

3. Traumatic Grief and Healing (a healing exploration)

2. The Wisdom of a Child

child loss

partners

sibling death

parent death

death-work

grief support & communities: your people

5. Grief & the Holidays: How to make your experience not stuck
10. Yoga & Grief: A match made in heaven
18. Guided by Grief: Lisa Bovee
21. Surviving Siblings: Kellyn Shoecraft (also has Surviving Parents)
22. Grief is … Heike Mertiins
27. John Pavlovitz on Death & Grief
28. Modern Loss: Cofounder Rebecca Soffer shares her story
30. Kate Manser: You Might Die Tomorrow (changed by death)
34. Death & Divinity
44. Reimagining Grief: Lisa Keefauver
48. After Chloe: The Story
54. Walking Her Mother Home: Kristie Bennett
56. Complex Trauma & Grief: Lindsay Joy
62. Grief Dreams with Dr. Joshua Black
63. Full Circle: Stephanie Sprinkel's story from grief to grief coach
65. A Grief Warrior: Leslie Barber (husband)
68. Shauna Janz: Death of Grasshopper—grief as initiation to life
71. Grief Alchemy: Taurie Bednarski
73. Good Grievings: Thomas Biddulph
76. The Memory Circle: Barri Leiner Grant
78. The Heart of a Grieving Child: Grief & Grits
79. My Story of Stillbirth & Miscarriage: Amy Watson
82. The Long Walk Home: Find your Harbor
84. Awakened by Death: Naila
81. Gentle Death with Dr. Annetta Mallon
85. Loving & Living your way through grief: Emily Thiroux Threatt
    (two husbands)
87. Grief: A Love Story with Tara Caffelle
89. Kellie Curtain: What Will I Wear to your Funeral
90. Your Faithful Griever: Miriam Wasmund
91. The Grave Woman: Jo'el Simone Anthony
94. Evolve beyond Grief: Susan Kendal
95. Spirituality & Grief: Dr. Terri Daniel
96. Grow with Grief: Katrina Weller
98. Dignity with Departure: Shantell Riley
100. Relaxing into the Pain: Dr. Mekel Harris
102. Oceana Sawyer: End of Life Doula

the beyond

(Almost every episode has an element of someone mentioning contact from beyond as that is a frequent question asked.)

keeping your loved one's body home

233

coming soon ...

Want to hear more from Becky Aud-Jennison? You're in luck! Her next book, *and the stars spoke: a memoir through the lens of death*, will be available May 10, 2022, everywhere books are sold.